CITY
LIFE IN THE BIG CITY

KURT BUSIEK
WRITER

BRENT E. ANDERSON
ARTIST

RICHARD STARKINGS
(AND) **COMICRAFT'S**
JOHN ROSHELL
LETTERING & DESIGN

STEVE BUCCELLATO
AND **ELECTRIC CRAYON**
COLOR ART

ALEX ROSS
COVERS

BUSIEK, ANDERSON & ROSS
ARCHITECTS & CITY PLANNERS

PRODUCTIONS

ANN HUNTINGTON BUSIEK
Managing Editor

RICHARD STARKINGS
Art Director

Jonathan Peterson	Editor-Original Series
Kristy Quinn	Editor
Ian Sattler	Director Editorial, Special Projects & Archival Editions
Robbin Brosterman	Design Director-Books
Eddie Berganza	Executive Editor
Bob Harras	VP—Editor in Chief
Diane Nelson	President
Dan DiDio and Jim Lee	Co-Publishers
Geoff Johns	Chief Creative Officer
John Rood	Executive VP—Sales, Marketing and Business Development
Amy Genkins	Senior VP—Business and Legal Affairs
Nairi Gardiner	Senior VP—Finance
Jeff Boison	VP—Publishing Operations
Mark Chiarello	VP—Art Direction and Design
John Cunningham	VP—Marketing
Terri Cunningham	VP—Talent Relations and Services
Alison Gill	Senior VP—Manufacturing and Operations
David Hyde	VP—Publicity
Hank Kanalz	Senior VP—Digital
Jay Kogan	VP—Business and Legal Affairs, Publishing
Jack Mahan	VP—Business Affairs, Talent
Nick Napolitano	VP—Manufacturing Administration
Ron Perazza	VP—Online
Sue Pohja	VP—Book Sales
Courtney Simmons	Senior VP—Publicity
Bob Wayne	Senior VP—Sales

ASTRO CITY: LIFE IN THE BIG CITY, published by DC Comics, 1700 Broadway, New York, NY 10019.
Cover Copyright © 2011, introduction, sketches and compilation Copyright © 1995, 1996 Juke Box
Productions. All Rights Reserved. Astro City, its logos, symbols, prominent characters featured in this
issue and the distinctive likenesses thereof are trademarks of Juke Box Productions.

Originally published by WildStorm as Kurt Busiek's Astro City Volume 1 #1-6. DC Comics and logo
are trademarks of DC Comics. Any similiarity to institutions or persons living or dead is unintentional
and purely coincidental. Printed on recyclable paper. DC Comics does not read or accept unsolicited
submissions of ideas, stories or artwork. Printed by RR Donnelley, Salem, VA, USA. 8/5/11.

DC Comics, a Warner Bros. Entertainment Company.

Hardcover ISBN: 978-1-4012-3261-0
Softcover ISBN: 978-1-4012-3262-7

CITYSCAPE BY
ART NICHOLS

CHAPTER DIVIDER FIGURES BY
CURT SWAN &   GEORGE TUSKA   JIM   JOHN
MURPHY ANDERSON   & JOE SINNOTT   MOONEY   ROMITA, SR.

Kurt
Busiek's

ASTRO

INTRODUCTION

 LOVE SUPERHEROES.
This comes as no surprise to
those who know me — I've been writing superhero comics professionally
for well over a decade and reading
them for even longer, and while superheroes haven't been all I've written (or
read), there'd be no point in denying
that I'm having a great time among the
folks in the capes and masks, and that I
have no intention of leaving them
behind any time soon.

Unfortunately, at least from my
perspective, the superhero is not as
well regarded by many of those
around me — friends, family, fellow
creators and a vocal number of comics
readers. I hear that there are too
many superheroes, that they're choking the racks and shelves of the comic
book stores, that they're the reason
comics are so poorly regarded by the
majority of Americans, and more. And
while I could quibble with some of the
above — I'd certainly like to see more
diversity of the comics racks, for
instance, but when I see superheroes
from Batman to Superman to Spider-
Man, the X-Men, the Teenage Mutant
Ninja Turtles, the Mighty Morphin
Power Rangers, the Crow, the Tick and
more in movies, on TV, in cartoons, in
books or blowing off the toy-store
shelves, I wonder whether superheroes are *really* what non-comics-
readers are turning up their noses at
when they pass up comic books — it's
one specific complaint against the
superhero that I want to bring up
here.

The complaint, which never fails
to charm me, is that superheroes are
limited. They're inherently juvenile, I'm
told. They're simplistic. They're just an
adolescent male power fantasy, a cryp-
to-fascist presentation of status quo
values, elevated over anything strange
or alien.

And sure, yeah, I can see that. Superman is adolescence personified — Clark Kent the weak child whom nobody takes seriously, turning into the powerful, respected (and sexually attractive, but nervous around women) Superman as swiftly as a teenager's voice cracks, and then back again to meek, unimportant Clark. Spider-Man is adolescence from a different angle — the teenager stumbling toward adulthood writ large, making mistakes with disastrous consequences and doing his best to remedy them as he learns to be a responsible man in an adult society. Captain America is the American ideal and self-image circa 1941 rolled into one — the biggest kid in the global playground, who's going to make the other kids play nice, even if he has to get a little rough to do it. I can absolutely see that.

However — and you knew there was going to be a however, right? — what charms me about that objection to the superhero is the way it points out, in the guise of criticism, what to me is the greatest strength of the superhero genre — the ease with which superheroes can be used as metaphor, as symbol, whether for the psychological transformation of adolescence, the self-image of a nation, or something else. A genre that can do something like that — is that really a limitation?

I don't think so.

If a superhero can be such a powerful and effective metaphor for male adolescence, then what else can you do with them? Could you build a superhero story around a metaphor for female adolescence? Around mid-life crisis? ※ Around the changes adults go through when they become parents? Sure, why not? And if a superhero can exemplify America's self-image at the dawn of World War II, could a superhero exemplify America's self-image during the less-confident 1970s? ※ ※ How about the emerging national identity of a newly-independent African nation? Or a non-national culture, like the drug culture, or the "greed-is-good" business culture of the go-go Eighties? Of course. If it can do one, it can do the others.

I could go on, but I'll spare you. The point is, an attempt to describe how limited superheroes are quickly turns into the question, "What *can't* they do?" The possibilities of the genre are endless, and the terrain rich and inviting.

THIS IS THE SORT OF THING that was running through my head when I first started working on ASTRO CITY. The superhero genre has historically been limited to adventure thrillers, action stories that can be sold easily to boys in their teen years or younger. But that's a self-imposed, market-driven limitation, not any sort of creative limitation of the genre, and I wanted to explore the *rest* of the genre, celebrating the power it has to make ideas come to life and seeing what it can do. I've long been fascinated by the question of *what else* happens in the worlds the superheroes inhabit; what life is like for the guy who points upward and declaims, "Look! Up in the sky!"; what celebrity posters are on the walls of 13-year-old girls in the Human Torch's world; what it's like for a lawyer to go into court and argue that his client is not guilty of murder because the killer was in fact his evil twin (and trot out all the precedents for such an event). This seemed to be a perfect chance to do both — to wander off the main thoroughfares of a superhero world and see what stories have been waiting in the shadows to be told, what chords can be struck, what we can discover if we stop heeding the siren song of What Happens Next and start wondering What Else Is There? I like What Happens Next stories just fine, as it happens, and I have plenty of venues to tell those — but not many in which I can pick out an innocent bystander at a slugfest between a superhero and a super-criminal, follow him or her home and see what's worth examining about this particular life. What resonates with our own experience? What cobwebbed, dusty corners can we illuminate?

One thing I didn't want to do is take the superhero story and make it "realistic" — which is odd, since that's become the quickie shorthand description of ASTRO CITY (and of MARVELS before it) that I've heard time and again: It's what superheroes would be like in the real world.

Well, no. No, it isn't.

We've got trolls living underground in Astro City. We've got time travelers reweaving the future. We've got fantastic technology, mystical creatures, alien contact and powerful, violent, destructive beings by the double handful — and in Astro City history, they've been around for decades, without turning the world into something unrecognizable from our own perspective. The telephone and the airplane may have transformed our world, but the superhero and the sorcerer haven't had anywhere near as great an effect in the world of Astro City. And I like it that way. Making a superhero world realistic — making it a hermetically-logical alternate reality in which all the pieces make sense and work logically — that strikes me less as a superhero story per se, and more as that branch of science fiction that gets its stories out of making some change in the world, and then extrapolating from it, exploring the ramifications of a change in technology, or history, or politics on all other aspects of the world. *How would the world be different*, this type of story asks, and while it's a perfectly valid form of fiction, I'm just not interested.

One of the most charming elements of the superhero story, for me, lies in the fact that the world it all happens in is our world — that this fantastic, furious, cosmic stuff happens in what could be the skies over our heads — and sure, it should transform the world into something unrecognizable, but it doesn't, not any more than the prevalence of court wizards or of multiple intelligent humanoid races sharing the same environment changes the politics or commerce of a fairy-tale world. I *like* the absurd, unrealistic glory of the superhero genre, and I want to see it as a place of gods and aliens and super-science and talking gorillas and ordinary people like you and me, all dealing with metaphor run amok, coping not with what *logical* effect it all has, but with the *emotional* effect. Not what it would *be* like if superheroes existed in our world, but what it would *feel* like if we could wander through theirs. It's not a realistic world, but it's a fascinating one.

ANOTHER REASON I'M HAPPY to let the world of Astro City be thoroughly unrealistic is that I think it's about time. For the past decade, starting around the time of the brilliant WATCHMEN and THE DARK KNIGHT RETURNS, the prevalent mode for "serious" superhero creators has been deconstruction. The superhero has been dissected, analyzed and debunked, his irrationalities held up to the light to show them for the unworkable Rube Goldberg machines they are, that it's almost become impossible to present a superhero who does what he does without being emotionally unstable, incapable of dealing with reality without "acting out" his psychoses and obsessions. But it strikes me that the only real reason to take apart a pocket watch, or a car engine, aside from the simple delight of disassembly, is to find out how it works. To understand it, so that you can put it back together again better than before, or build a new one that goes beyond what the old model could do.

We've been taking apart the superhero for ten years or more; it's time to put it back together and wind it up, time to take it out on the road and floor it, see what it'll do. That's the prospect that excites me, that makes me eager to tell my stories to anyone who's willing to listen. Where can we go from here? What's out there to find? Come on, let's head that way — all we can see are shapes in the dark, but they sure look interesting, don't they?

I'VE BEEN EXTREMELY LUCKY in all this. Lucky to have done MARVELS at just the right time, winning me enough of an audience and a reputation to allow me to launch ASTRO CITY. Lucky to have worked with Alex Ross, whose devotion to archetype and emotional power birthed MARVELS, and whose consummate skill brought readers flocking to the project — and who brings the same commitment and skill to striking just the right image with the ASTRO CITY covers. Lucky to work with Brent Anderson, who can draw anything I throw at him, and who's willing to do whatever it takes to make the story come to life on the page. And lucky that neither Brent nor Alex is content to just "do the job" — they've contributed ideas, shaped characters and settings, argued me out of mistakes, fought for their vision and the good of the stories and been fully engaged in making ASTRO CITY a reality; without them I might have a book, but it wouldn't be anywhere near as good. The same can be said for Richard Starkings and John Gaushell of Comicraft, whose design skills and technical expertise have made ASTRO CITY a clean, crisp package; for Steve Buccellato and Electric Crayon, who gave the stories life and mood and power in their color work; and for Image Comics, who gave us a shot at telling our stories as best we could, helping us reach an audience without trying to exert any creative control.

There are no talking gorillas in the stories that follow (we'll get to them, honest). But looking back on them, I think we did what we set out to do — we told the stories we wanted to tell with as much honesty and as much skill as we could muster, and let them out into the world to fly or fall. They seem, for the most part, to have flown.

Welcome to Astro City. Whether you're getting to know the place for the first time, or are a regular commuter, I hope you enjoy wandering its streets and seeing its sights as much as we have.

— *Kurt Busiek*
MAY 1996

❋ IN FACT, IT'S ALREADY BEEN DONE. DO YOURSELF A FAVOR AND HUNT DOWN A COPY OF *SUPERFOLKS*, BY ROBERT N. MAYER [DIAL PRESS, 1977], A NOVEL THAT BRILLIANTLY USES SUPERHERO SYMBOLS TO TELL A SIDESPLITTINGLY FUNNY AND EMOTIONALLY AFFECTING STORY OF A MAN DEALING WITH MIDDLE AGE; IT'S LONG OUT OF PRINT BUT IT'S WELL WORTH THE TROUBLE OF FINDING IT.

❋ ❋ THE KINKS USE CAPTAIN AMERICA TO DO JUST THAT, IN THEIR SONG, "CATCH ME NOW I'M FALLING," ON THE ALBUM *LOW BUDGET*.

CHAPTER 1

IN MY DREAMS I FLY.

IN DREAMS

I SOAR *UNFETTERED* AND *SERENE*, LAUGHING AT GRAVITY AND AT *CARE*.

THE CLOUDS *EMBRACE* ME AS A FRIEND AND THE WIND LAZILY *TOUSLES* MY HAIR.

I *LOSE* MYSELF IN THE SUN AND SKY.

AMAGAMGANGGANGTEK

THE *ALARM CLOCK* --

-- NO, *NOT* THE ALARM CLOCK. IT HASN'T HAD A CHANCE TO RING IN *YEARS.*

THE *EMERGENCY ALERT TRANSMITTER.* AS *ALWAYS.*

THE LIGHT STABS AT MY EYES AND I FEEL *HEAVY* AND *OLD.*

BUT THAT *CAN'T MATTER.*

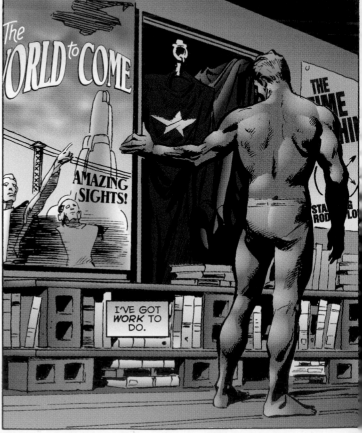

The WORLD to COME

AMAZING SIGHTS!

I'VE GOT *WORK* TO DO.

THE PULSE-PATTERN OF THE TRANSMISSION INDICATES THE PHILIPPINES.

SOME SORT OF WEATHER DISASTER -- PROBABLY ANOTHER TYPHOON.

MANILA'S A NICE FLIGHT, UNDER OTHER CIRCUMSTANCES. BUT NOT TODAY.

THERE'S NO TIME.

THERE'S NEVER ANY TIME.

-- AND, HEADING BACK, *PYRAMID* ASSASSINS IN TURKEY AND A NASTY CHRONAL RIFT IN STUTTGART. A LOT OF MID-AIR ANTICS --

-- BUT IT'S NOT THE SAME THING AS *REAL* FLYING.

FOUR-PLUS HOURS OF WORK -- *SEVENTEEN SECONDS* OF FLIGHT --

-- AND I WALK INTO THE OFFICE WITH *MOMENTS* TO SPARE.

CURRENT ASTRO CITY WEEKLY FEATURE VERIFICATION DEPARTMENT

MORNING, ASA.

ASA.

RICH, KAREN, SHAKIRA -- WHAT'S THE *GOOD WORD?*

ASTRO CITY ROCKET
JACK-IN-THE-BOX CAPTURES BRASS MONKEY

"DEADLINES," LIKE ALWAYS. FOUR MANUSCRIPTS LATE OUT OF EDITORIAL, AND *GUESS WHO* GETS TO MAKE UP THE TIME?

BE WARNED -- *LADY CAVENDISH* IS FLEXING HER *WHIP.*

WELL, IF THINGS ARE THAT DIRE, MIGHT AS WELL GET *TO IT.*

"*TIME NOR TIDE TARRIETH NO MAN.*"

HEYWOOD?

ROCKET
N-THE-BOX

ROBERT GREENE, DISPUTATIONS. YOU KNOW, FOR SOMEONE WHO ENJOYS HIS *JOB* SO MUCH --

"-- YOU FIGURE JUST ONCE HE'D GET HERE A LITTLE *EARLY...*

ASA MARTIN
VERIFICATION

19

ASIDE FROM YESTERDAY'S STUFF, I GET TWO NEW PIECES TO FACT-CHECK. THE FIRST FAMILY PIECE IS A *TRIPLE RUSH.*

FAMOUS "FIRSTS"
45 Years and Three Generations of Adventure

NOT BAD -- A LITTLE *FLORID,* BUT IT CAPTURES THE SUBJECT WELL.

I POWER THE *ZYXOMETER* UP, AND PROGRAM IT FOR THE MORNING'S WORK -- PHONE CALLS, REFERENCE CITES, REPORT GENERATION.

I ALREADY KNOW WHAT THE *ANSWERS* WILL BE, AND EVEN WHICH ERRORS WILL GO *UNCAUGHT* --

-- BUT THEY NEED THEIR *PROCEDURES* FOLLOWED. AND I NEED THEIR COMPUTER SYSTEM'S *NETWORK CONNECTIONS.*

BIPBIPBIPBIP

LOOKS LIKE IT'S GOING TO BE A *BUSY MORNING.*

THE ZYXOMETER CHANNELS OVER *75 NEWS SOURCES* -- RADIO, TV, THE NEWSWIRES -- AND RANKS CRISES BY *URGENCY.*

I DEAL WITH A *RUNAWAY BUS* IN MIDTOWN (LESS THAN A THIRD OF A SECOND TRAVEL TIME) --

-- AN ATTACK ON THE *DENVER CITY HALL* BY *DR. SATURDAY* (1.1 SECONDS) --

-- AND A NEAR-DISASTER AT *FBU'S BIO LABS* (HALF A SECOND, BUT ONLY TO AVOID THE AIRPORT).

THE IRREGULARS: SHOULDN'T THEY BE IN SCHOOL!

BACK AT WORK, I SHUFFLE SOME PAPERS, ADD A FEW HANDWRITTEN NOTES TO THE REPORTS --

-- GENERALLY MAKE THE OFFICE LOOK LIKE IT'S BEEN *USED* --

-- AND IT'S *LUNCHTIME*.

WE'RE GONNA CHECK OUT THAT NEW *CUBAN-CHINESE* PLACE, ASA -- WANNA JOIN US?

SORRY, CAN'T. *APPOINTMENTS* -- YOU KNOW HOW IT IS.

I SWEAR, I *USED* TO THINK HE WAS STANDOFFISH --

"-- BUT I'M STARTING TO BELIEVE HE REALLY *IS* THE BUSIEST GUY ON EARTH!"

HONOR GUARD HEADQUARTERS IS IN CAMOUFLAGE MODE OVER THE *MIDWEST* THIS WEEK, 2.7 SECONDS AWAY --

CUTTIN' IT A BIT *FINE*, EH, BIG RED? WE WERE GETTIN' READY T'START *WITHOUT YA!*

BUTTON IT, QUARREL. SAMARITAN'S NEVER MISSED A MEETING, WHICH IS MORE THAN I CAN SAY FOR YOU!

NOW, NOW. NO NEED TO *FUSS* -- WE'RE ALL HERE.

WE COMPARE *NOTES* -- WHO'S IN JAIL, WHO'S AT LARGE, WHO'S DISAPPEARED COMPLETELY.

CLEOPATRA REPORTS *GNOMES* MASSING IN THE MOUNTAINS. THE *BLACK RAPIER* THINKS *THE DEACON'S* UP TO SOMETHING.

I MENTION *PYRAMID* AND DR. SATURDAY.

THE ALIEN DETECTOR'S BEEN MALFUNCTIONING SINCE THE *ZONN* ATTACKS, SO WE FINALLY *OVERHAUL* IT.

BOOST POWER-FLOW BY *THIRTEEN PERCENT,* N-FORCER --

GOT IT.

-- *OKAY,* I SEE IT NOW.

CLEOPATRA *STILL* SAYS MAGIC IS MORE DEPENDABLE.

WE HAVE NO EXTRATERRESTRIAL MEMBERS AT THE MOMENT, SO WE HAVE TO CALIBRATE IT AGAINST M.P.H.'S *NERVOUS SYSTEM.*

SO, DOC, WHAT'S THE *VERDICT* -- WILL I EVER PLAY THE VIOLIN AGAIN?

PERFECT -- WE'RE READING 85% HUMAN WITH A 15% ALIEN OVERLAY.

-- AND LOOK! *ZERO* SENSE OF HUMOR!

THAT OUGHT TO HOLD, UNTIL WE CAN BORROW THE *XENOFORM* FROM LEAVENWORTH --

-- OR *BEAUTIE* BRINGS *THE TOURIST* BY.

I HOPE IT'S *THE XENOFORM.* I'D RATHER DEAL WITH THREE TONS OF MURDEROUS SHAPE-SHIFTING PROTOPLASM THAN THAT *EXTRATERRESTRIAL GADABOUT.*

MAYBE *TWO* XENOFORMS.

And of course, no Honor Guard meeting would be *complete* without an emergency.

HA! ENOUGH OF CIRCUITRY AND WIRING -- WE HAVE A *CALL TO ARMS!*

This time it's Astrobank's *City Center* branch (a luxurious *ten seconds*, waiting for the others) --

-- and the *Menagerie Gang.*

HONOR GUARD! WE'RE *SCREWED!*

BIG TIME.

NO! WE CAN TAKE 'EM! REMEMBER THE *CONTINGENCY PLAN!*

NO, TAKE IT FROM *ME* -- FOXIE LOXY IS *RIGHT.* YOU'RE *SCREWED.*

NICE *TALK,* THERE, QUARREL -- BUT I'M ALREADY *WAY AHEAD* OF YOU!

HAVE *AT YOU,* FELLAH!

It's almost *embarrassing,* we outmatch them so badly.

They'd picked up some sort of *enhanced ordnance,* but it doesn't make any difference.

They go *down* --

DIDN'T YOUR MOTHER EVER TELL YOU IT'S NOT *NICE* TO ROB BANKS?

YEAH, YEAH, BIG DEAL! LIKE WE DON'T ALREADY *KNOW* YOU'RE FAST...

-- AND, SECONDS AFTER THEY'RE SECURED --

BAM BAM

ASA MARTIN! YOU'D BETTER BE IN THERE! LUNCH HOUR ENDED TEN MINUTES AGO!

WITH YOU IN A *SEC*, MS. CAVENDISH --

-- AND HERE'S THE *FIRST FAMILY* PIECE FOR YOU.

-;HRMPH;- WELL. I *HAVE* TOLD YOU ABOUT LOCKING YOUR DOOR...

I KNOW, AND I'M *SORRY*. BUT THE SOLITUDE HELPS ME *WORK* FASTER.

WELL. YOU *ARE* OUR MOST EFFICIENT CHECKER, I'LL GRANT YOU THAT.

WHICH IS WHY I'M *HERE*. ANOTHER PIECE.

IT'S FOR *NEXT* WEEK, SO DON'T LET IT SIDE-TRACK YOU -- BUT IT REQUIRES *ABSOLUTE CONFIDENTIALITY*. THE OTHER MAGAZINES --

-- WELL, THEY'D *LOVE* TO STEAL A MARCH ON US --

MY REWARD FOR DOING A GOOD JOB. EXTRA WORK. PERHAPS I COULD HAVE THE ZYXOMETER MAKE A FEW *MISTAKES*...

-- SO I'M *COUNTING* ON YOU, ASA. I *KNOW* YOU'LL COME THROUGH.

...BUT *NO*. THAT WOULDN'T BE RIGHT.

24

I OPEN THE FOLDER TO SEE WHAT'S SO *CLASSIFIED* --

-- AND MY *HEART* SINKS.

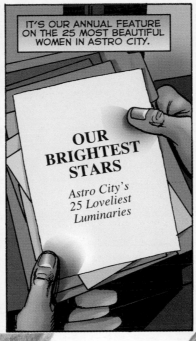

IT'S OUR ANNUAL FEATURE ON THE 25 MOST BEAUTIFUL WOMEN IN ASTRO CITY.

OUR BRIGHTEST STARS

Astro City's 25 Loveliest Luminaries

I *HATE* THIS PIECE. I HATE THE *PHOTOS,* ESPECIALLY -- THE EYES, THE LUSTROUS HAIR, THE PERFECT SKIN --

-- THE SATINS AND VELVETS --

-- REMINDING ME, *MOCKING* ME, WITH WHAT I'M GIVING UP.

BUT WHEN COULD I SPARE THE *TIME?* FOR FRIENDS. TO RELAX. FOR A *LIFE.*

-- AND WHO *AMONG* THEM WOULDN'T WANT TO MEET *SAMARITAN?* WHO AMONG THEM --

THESE WOMEN -- I HAVE THEIR *ADDRESSES,* PHONE NUMBERS, THEIR *WORK* SCHEDULES --

IT'S ALMOST A *RELIEF* WHEN THE ALERT SIGNAL GOES OFF.

BIPBIPBIPBIPBIPBIPBIPBIP

I FINISH PROGRAMMING THE ZYXOMETER FOR THE AFTERNOON'S TASKS, AND I LEAVE IT *TO* THEM.

THE AFTERNOON GOES BY --

-- A *JAILBREAK* AT *BIRO ISLAND* (LESS THAN A SECOND TO FLY THERE) --

-- HELPING THE MARITIME MUSEUM RAISE THE *SEA BLAZE*, SUNK IN 1665 OFF THE FLORIDA COAST (THREE SECONDS) --

-- AND A *FRIGHTENED* LITTLE BALL OF *ORANGE AND WHITE* ON CICERO STREET.

I SLOW DOWN (TWO SECONDS) TO LET THE LITTLE GIRL *SEE* ME CLEARLY AND REASSURE HER THAT IT'S ALL RIGHT --

-- AND IT ALMOST COSTS A MAN IN BOSTON HIS *LIFE*.

JESUS!

I MAKE A NOTE TO TRY NOT TO *WASTE TIME* LIKE THAT IN THE FUTURE --

-- AND I HOLD THE BUILDING TOGETHER WHILE THEY *EVACUATE* IT.

I CAN'T SAVE EVERYBODY -- PEOPLE DIE EVEN WHILE I'M SAVING LIVES HERE -- BUT I CAN STILL DO WHAT I *CAN.*

CAN'T I?

IT TURNS OUT THE BUILDING WAS BOMBED TO *DRAW* POLICE ATTENTION WHILE THE MAYOR WAS BEING *KIDNAPPED.*

ONCE EVACUATION'S COMPLETE, I *BRING* IN THE KIDNAPPERS AND HEAD BACK TO THE OFFICE FOR A LATE *WRAP-UP* --

-- AND IN TIME TO GET READY FOR *DINNER.*

TONIGHT, IT'S THE *FIREFIGHTERS ASSOCIATION.*

-- WITH THE *GREATEST HONOR,* AND *DEEPEST* SENSE OF *GRATITUDE,* THAT I *PRESENT* THIS TOKEN OF OUR ESTEEM TO THE MAN WHO --

I TRIED ONCE TO SIMPLY *IGNORE* THESE EVENTS, BUT IT OFFENDED PEOPLE --

-- *GREAT HONOR.* I *THANK* YOU, AND WILL CONTINUE TO DO MY BEST, FOR THE PEOPLE OF *ASTRO CITY* AND THE ENTIRE --

-- AS IF I WAS SAYING I WAS *TOO GOOD* FOR THEM.

SO I SMILE, AND EAT THE CHICKEN --

-- AND EXCUSE MYSELF *TWICE* DURING DINNER TO DEAL WITH CRISES.

CLAP CLAP CLAP CLAP CLAP CLAP CLAP CLAP CLAP CLAP

AFTERWARD, I SHAKE MY HOSTS' HANDS AND AUTOGRAPH HELMETS AND REITERATE THAT IT'S *THEY* WHO ARE THE TRUE HEROES --

-- AND THEY *ARE*, THERE'S NOT A SHRED OF DOUBT ABOUT THAT --

-- AND IN THE NEAREST ALLEYWAY, I LET MY MIND GO BLANK AND LET THE DAY'S TENSION DRAIN FROM MY BODY.

I REACH THE STATE OF CALM *NECESSARY* FOR THE SHIFT --

-- AND TAKE A STEP *SIDEWAYS.*

THE "CLOSET" IS JUST AS I LEFT IT, EXCEPT FOR MORE *MICROSPORE BUILDUP.* IT MAY BE THE LOCAL EQUIVALENT OF HOUSE DUST --

-- BUT YOU NEVER *KNOW.* I'LL ASK THE *N-FORCER* ABOUT IT NEXT WEEK.

AND THAT SHOULD BE *IT* --

ACFA

PRESENTED BY THE
ASTRO CITY FIREFIGHTERS ASSOCIATION
WITH GRATITUDE AND RESPECT, TO
SAMARITAN
AUGUST 8, 1995

-- EXCEPT IT NEVER *IS.*

KAWHAMM!!

30

IT *RAMS* THROUGH MY *EMPYREAN WEB* LIKE THERE'S *NOTHING THERE.*

THE *LIVING NIGHTMARE* WAS CREATED YEARS AGO BY A PSYCHOLOGIST WHO TRIED TO *ELIMINATE FEAR.*

HRAH!

INSTEAD, ALL HE DID WAS *EXTERNALIZE* IT --

HARR!

-- CREATING A *VIOLENT, DESTRUCTIVE CREATURE* THAT LASHES OUT AT ANYTHING THAT *THREATENS* IT.

OVER THE YEARS, THE NIGHTMARE'S TAKEN *MANY FORMS* --

KRAKK

-- EVEN TWICE, WITH A *MARINE PILOT'S* MIND SUPERSEDING THE CREATURE'S *CONSCIOUSNESS,* BECOMING A MEMBER OF *HONOR GUARD.*

THESE DAYS, IT'S IN AN *EXCEPTIONALLY ANNOYING* CONFIGURATION.

RUU?

IT APPEARS OUT OF *NOWHERE* --

-- IT'S *DRAWN* TO THE SUPER-POWERED BEINGS THAT HAVE SO OFTEN *CONTAINED* IT --

-- AND IT *LEECHES* OFF OUR ENERGY, SO THAT I CAN'T HARM IT --

THAK

NF!

-- AND EVERY TIME I HIT IT I GROW *WEAKER.*

AND IT ALWAYS -- *ALWAYS!* -- ATTACKS WHEN I'M TIRED.

THAT MAY BE A *FUNCTION* OF ITS CURRENT INCARNATION -- I DON'T KNOW.

GRAAHH!

I'LL HAVE TO TAKE THAT UP WITH *DR. PROCHNOW.* PROVIDED I SURVIVE THIS.

ONE THING I'LL SAY FOR THE NIGHTMARE, THOUGH --

GARRARRAR!

-- IT'S *DEPENDABLY STUPID*. I FINALLY MANEUVER IT DIRECTLY ON *TOP* OF ME --

-- AND FROM THERE, IT'S *EASY*.

BRARGH!

THE TRIP INTO ORBIT DOESN'T LAST *LONG ENOUGH* FOR IT TO DRAIN ME TOO BADLY --

-- AND THERE'S NOTHING IT CAN *HURT* BETWEEN HERE AND THE SUN.

BUT SURE ENOUGH, IT BLINKS OUT OF *EXISTENCE* AS SOON AS IT'S FAR ENOUGH AWAY FROM THE EMOTIONS THAT *POWER* IT.

IN SOME WAYS, THAT'S THE MOST *FRUSTRATING* PART OF THE ENTIRE BATTLE.

I'D LIKE TO TAKE MY TIME HEADING BACK. I'M BRUISED, EXHAUSTED, AND EARTH IS SO LOVELY BY STARLIGHT.

BUT THERE'S PROPERTY DAMAGE TO DEAL WITH, A GAS MAIN TO REPAIR, WOUNDED TO ATTEND TO AND MORE.

IT'S PAST ONE A.M. BY THE TIME I GET BACK TO MY APARTMENT.

I TALLY UP THE DAY.

FIFTY-SIX SECONDS. BEST DAY SINCE MARCH.

I'M SLIPPING AWAY BEFORE MY HEAD HITS THE PILLOW.

AND I SLEEP --

-- AND I
DREAM --

CHAPTER 2

"THE SALARY'S **ACCEPTABLE,** THEN?"

ROCKET!

GETCHER MORNING **ROCKET!**

UH, YES -- YES, IT'S **FINE.**

GOOD. THEN WELCOME TO THE **ASTRO CITY ROCKET,** SON. I EXPECT **GREAT THINGS** FROM YOU.

I'LL TRY TO **LIVE UP** TO THAT, MISTER MILLS.

PLEASE, IT'S **ELLIOT.** I'M ONLY "**MISTER MILLS**" WHEN YOU'VE DONE SOMETHING WRONG.

UH, YES SIR, MISTER-- I MEAN, **ELLIOT.**

DON'T **WORRY,** KID. I'M NOT GOING TO **BITE** YOU.

I HAD SALLY MAKE US LUNCH RESERVATIONS AT THE PRESS CLUB. I'LL INTRODUCE YOU TO SOME OF THE GUYS YOU'LL BE WORKING WITH.

THAT **ALL RIGHT** WITH **YOU?**

THE **PRESS CLUB?** THAT...THAT'LL BE FINE!

GOOD. WE'VE GOT A FEW MINUTES BEFORE IT'S TIME TO HEAD DOWN, THEN.

RELAX. LOOSEN YOUR **TIE,** MAYBE -- YOU LOOK LIKE YOU'RE **CHOKING.**

THANK YOU, SIR.

39

UH, SIR?

ELLIOT.

ELLIOT MILLS

SORRY. THIS *ARTICLE* YOU'VE GOT FRAMED HERE. I CAN UNDERSTAND WHY ALL THE *OTHERS* --

-- BUT WHY THIS ONE?

YOU'RE OBSERVANT. I *LIKE* THAT. THAT'S A STORY I USUALLY TELL OVER LUNCH, BUT I THINK THE CLUB WAITERS ARE GETTING *TIRED* OF IT.

IF YOU'D LIKE TO HEAR IT *NOW*...

OF COURSE, SURE!

ONE OR THE OTHER, SON. "OF COURSE" OR "SURE." *BOTH* IS REDUNDANT.

BUT NEVER MIND. HAVE A SEAT. LET ME SET THE *STAGE* FOR YOU...

WORLD'S FINEST GRANDD

"I WAS A LOT LIKE YOU -- A KID RIGHT OUT OF JOURNALISM SCHOOL, NEW TO THE CITY. I HAD A NEW JOB -- A GIRL --

"-- AND THE WORLD AROUND ME WAS FRESH AND VITAL. THERE WAS SPIRIT, AND COMMUNITY --

"-- A SENSE THAT WE WERE ALL PULLING TOGETHER. FOR THE SPACE RACE -- FOR DEMOCRACY --

"-- WHATEVER WAS GOING ON IN THE WORLD --

"-- WE WERE A PART OF IT."

HUH --?

MOVE! MOVE!

WHAT IS --

OH LORD --!

BLAM

BLAM

"WE WERE A PART OF IT --"

WHAT?!

WHO --?

PKAFF

PKAFF

PKAFF

"MY PLACE IN THAT WORLD WAS 'REPORTER,' THOUGH I HADN'T REALLY REPORTED ANYTHING YET.

"IT WAS MY JOB TO TELL THE PEOPLE WHAT WAS HAPPENING *AROUND* THEM.

"AND *LORD*, HOW I WANTED TO TELL THEM THAT *PARTICULAR* STORY --"

PRESS! PRESS! I NEED THAT *PHONE!*

TELEPH

HUH? SURE, NO *PROBLEM* --

OPERATOR -- GET ME THE *ROCKET* -- THE CITY ROOM!

KLIKA KLIK

"BUT IT WASN'T TO BE, NOT THAT TIME..."

PRESS

ASTRO CITY ROCKET

"-- WE WERE ALL HUNGRY FOR A BREAK. TO *DO* SOMETHING. TO *MATTER*."

YOU'LL *GET* YOUR STORY, HONEY. YOU'RE *GOOD*. I CAN SEE IT.

WELL, AT LEAST *SOMEONE'S* GOT FAITH IN ME.

I'D SNEAK YOU UP, BUT I'VE GOT AN *EARLY* AUDITION TOMORROW.

ANOTHER RADIO JINGLE, OR A *SOAP* THIS TIME?

Rooms to Let to Ladies.

NO, A PLAY -- A *REAL* PLAY!

THEY'VE GOT NO *MONEY*, OF COURSE -- THEY'RE PUTTING IT ON IN A COFFEEHOUSE --

-- BUT OH, YOU SHOULD SEE THE *SCRIPT!*

"IT WAS LIKE *ELECTRICITY* OR SOMETHING -- FOR ALL OF US.

"WE COULD *FEEL* IT OUT THERE, WAITING. WAITING FOR EACH OF US TO REACH OUT AND TAKE A *HOLD* OF IT.

"AND THEN I CAUGHT THE *FLICKER* -- NOT A SPARK, BUT *FURTIVE MOVEMENT* --

"-- I HAD MY OPPORTUNITY TO *REACH OUT* --

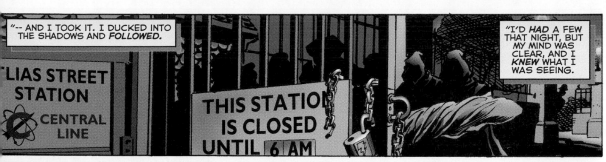

"-- AND I TOOK IT. I DUCKED INTO THE SHADOWS AND *FOLLOWED.*

"I'D *HAD* A FEW THAT NIGHT, BUT MY MIND WAS CLEAR, AND I *KNEW* WHAT I WAS SEEING.

LIAS STREET STATION

⚛ CENTRAL LINE

THIS STATION IS CLOSED UNTIL 6 AM

"ROBED MEN -- LIKE *MONKS* OR SOMETHING. DEFINITELY A *STORY* -- A BIGGER STORY THAN A *FLOWER SHOW*, AT ANY RATE.

"THE MEN WERE CAUTIOUS. QUIET. THEY OBVIOUSLY DIDN'T WANT TO BE *SEEN* --

"-- AND *NO WONDER!*"

THE ALTAR -- *THERE!*

IN THE MIDDLE OF THE *TRACKS?*

THERE WON'T BE A TRAIN FOR ANOTHER *SIX MINUTES*, ACOLYTE -- MORE THAN ENOUGH TIME!

NOW *SILENCE* -- I BEGIN!

By the power of the dark heart -- of blood and bone crushed to powder --

-- by the power of the killing fish --

-- the great fish that never rests, whose hunger is never sated --

-- by the power of the relentless destroyer --

-- I call on you, O mighty one --

-- I call to you across the gulf of worlds and the tides of space --

"-- AND IN THE PRESENCE OF *SOMETHING ELSE* "

I THANK YOU, KARNUS. YOUR WORLD IS NOW WITHIN STRIKING DISTANCE.

YOU AND YOUR MINNOWS HAVE SERVED ME WELL --

-- AND YOU SHALL NOT GO UNREWARDED!

TAKE MY POWER UNTO YOU -- TAKE MY HUNGER AS YOUR OWN --

-- AND RISE --

-- RISE AS THE NEWEST RAVAGERS IN THE ARMY OF **SHIRAK** THE **DEVOURER!**

YOUR ARMY'S NOT GOING ANYWHERE EXCEPT THE *STOCKADE*, CHUM!

BRAVE TALK, LITTLE *SILVER-SCALED MACKEREL* --

-- BUT YOU CANNOT HOPE TO PREVAIL AGAINST SHIRAK'S ARMY ALONE!

COULD BE YOU'RE *RIGHT*, SHIRAK --

"THE *HONOR GUARD.* IT HAD ONLY BEEN A FEW *WEEKS* SINCE THEY'D BEEN FORMED -- SINCE *MAX O'MILLIONS* HAD RALLIED THE WORLD'S GREATEST HEROES, *OLD* AND *NEW,* AGAINST THE *LEGIONS OF MIDNIGHT.* WE DIDN'T EVEN KNOW IF THEY'D BE STAYING *TOGETHER.*

"BUT THERE THEY WERE, RALLIED AROUND THE AGENT: *MAX, CLEOPATRA, LEOPARDMAN* AND *KITKAT, STARWOMAN,* THE *N-FORCER...*

"...EVEN THE *BOUNCING BEATNIK* WAS THERE..."

FEAR *NOT*, OBSERVER. THIS BATTLE IS *FAR* FROM OVER.

H-HUH?

"I COULD HAVE SWORN IT WAS *SOLID ROCK* BEHIND ME.

"BUT ALL OF A SUDDEN HE WAS *THERE*. MOVING PAST ME, STRIDING TOWARD THE BATTLE CALMLY, UNHURRIEDLY.

"BUT ONE LOOK AT THAT *LINED, WEATHERED FACE*, AND I KNEW WHO IT WAS."

"NO ONE HAD SEEN HIM SINCE *1944*. BUT HE'D BEEN THOUGHT DEAD BEFORE -- IN *1918*, IN *1898*, IN *1863*.

THE OLD SOLDIER.

"WHATEVER I'D THOUGHT -- WHATEVER I'D *FEARED* -- IF IT WAS BAD ENOUGH TO REQUIRE HIS PRESENCE --"

AGENT

"-- IT WAS WORSE THAN I COULD *POSSIBLY* IMAGINE."

WE ARE IN A *HALF-WORLD* BETWEEN REALITIES -- AND WE MUST PREVENT IT FROM BECOMING A *BEACHHEAD!*

KNOW YOU *THIS* --

"I'D NEVER SEEN HIM MYSELF, OF COURSE. THERE'S NO FILM FOOTAGE OF HIM, NO *PHOTOGRAPHS*.

ELLIOT, WHERE'VE YOU *BEEN*? WHEN YOU DIDN'T SHOW UP AT *WORK*, THEY CALLED, AND --

I'LL TELL YOU LATER. I HAVE TO *WRITE*.

"AN ATTACK ON HUMANITY"? WHAT *IS* THIS?

YOU GOT A *STORY*, ELLIOT?

THE SILVER AGENT? *HONOR GUARD*?

A *SHARK*?

SHIRAK THE *WHAT*?

THE *BOUNCING BEATNIK*?!

PULL THE *OTHER* ONE, GUY -- THE BEATNIK'S NOT PART OF HONOR GUARD!

MAX WOULD *NEVER* WORK WITH HIM...

THE OLD SOLDIER? NOT A *CHANCE*.

APRIL FOOL'S DAY WAS *MONTHS* AGO, ELLIOT...

HEY! IF ELLIOT SAYS IT HAPPENED, IT *HAPPENED*!

DON'T YOU *SAY* THINGS LIKE THAT!

I *CAN'T*, ELLIOT. IT'S *UNSUPPORTABLE.*

BUT -- IT *HAPPENED!* WE WERE UNDER *ATTACK* -- THEY WOULD HAVE *INVADED* US --

WHAT?! WHAT DO YOU *MEAN* YOU'RE NOT RUNNING IT!

I'VE READ IT, I'VE *READ* IT. BUT IT'S COMPLETELY *UNSOURCED.* YOU HAVE NO *WITNESSES.*

I WAS *THERE!* I SAW IT *ALL!*

THE AGENT, THE SHARK-MEN, THE *OLD SOLDIER* -- HE WAS CLOSE ENOUGH FOR ME TO *TOUCH!*

I WAS *THERE!*

NO OFFENSE, ELLIOT. BUT A *NEOPHYTE REPORTER,* HIS FIRST WEEK ON THE JOB, BRINGING IN A *WILD STORY* LIKE THIS --

-- EXTRA-DIMENSIONAL ATTACK, MYSTIC HALF-WORLDS, THE *OLD SOLDIER...*

...WOULD *YOU* BELIEVE IT, IN MY SHOES?

BUT -- BUT --

REWRITE IT, ELLIOT. REWRITE IT --

-- AND STICK TO THE FACTS YOU CAN *BACK UP.*

59

"SO I REWROTE IT --"

NO ONE'S EVER *HEARD* OF ANY SHARK-CULT. THE OLD SOLDIER'S BEEN DEAD FOR *FIFTEEN YEARS.*

"-- AND I REWROTE IT --"

IF WE COULD *CONTACT* ANY OF HONOR GUARD -- VERIFY EVEN A *PIECE* OF THIS --

"-- AND I REWROTE IT --"

LOOK, ELLIOT. STOP TRYING TO BE A *DETECTIVE.* BE A *REPORTER.* YOU HAVE SOME FACTS HERE. HARD *FACTS.*

VERIFY THEM, AND *THAT'S* YOUR PIECE. NOW DON'T COME BACK UNTIL YOU'VE DONE IT *RIGHT.*

SO I DID IT. I MADE THE PHONE CALLS, I *WROTE* THE PIECE --

-- AND IT WENT INTO THE *EVENING EDITION.* JUST AS YOU READ IT.

WORLD FINES GRANDD

THAT -- THAT'S *IT?* THAT'S HOW IT ENDS? BUT YOUR STORY -- WHAT YOU WROTE THE *FIRST* TIME --

-- YOUR FRIENDS AT THE BAR -- YOUR GIRLFRIEND -- WHAT DID THEY *SAY?*

OH, I WAS IN THE *DOGHOUSE*. THEY LAUGHED AT ME FOR *MONTHS*. EVEN LESLIE -- SHE NEVER *SAID* ANYTHING, BUT I COULD TELL.

REMEMBER, HONOR GUARD HAD NO HEADQUARTERS THEN, NO *PRESS SECRETARY*. I COULDN'T CONFIRM THE STORY FOR *YEARS* --

-- AND BY THEN, BOTH *SHIRAK* AND THE *SOLDIER* HAD TURNED UP AGAIN.

WOW -- THE DEVOURER *FIVE YEARS* EARLY. THE OLD SOLDIER RETURNING *BEFORE* THE FALL OF SAIGON.

IT MUST HAVE BEEN *INCREDIBLY* FRUSTRATING FOR YOU.

OH, IT *WAS*. I CARRIED THAT ARTICLE WITH ME FOR YEARS, AND ONCE I BECAME AN EDITOR, I HAD IT *FRAMED*.

AS A REMINDER THAT *HIDEBOUND EDITING* CAN STIFLE THE NEWS?

NO, THOUGH THAT'S WHAT MOST PEOPLE *THINK* WHEN THEY HEAR THE STORY.

NO -- I SAVED THE ARTICLE BECAUSE HE WAS *RIGHT*.

NOW, C'MON -- TIME FOR *LUNCH*. I'M STARVED, HOW ABOUT YOU?

BUT -- WHAT YOU *SAW* --

THIS IS A STRANGE WORLD, SON, AND THERE ARE LOTS OF *WEIRD THINGS* IN IT. THAT MAKES US, AS A NEWSPAPER, *VULNERABLE*.

OTHER NEWSPAPERS MAY GO OUT THERE WITH *SENSATIONAL* STORIES, *SCREAMING* HEADLINES THAT TURN OUT TO BE A MISTAKE --

-- AND THEY END UP LOOKING LIKE *MONKEYS*. NOT US.

HERE AT THE *ROCKET,* WE PRINT WHAT WE CAN *PROVE.* SOMETIMES IT'S *SPECTACULAR,* AND SOMETIMES IT *ISN'T* --

-- BUT OUR READERS *COUNT* ON US. AND SPECTACULAR OR NOT, THEY *KNOW* -- IF THEY READ IT IN THE *ROCKET* --

-- IT'S THE *TRUTH.*

Trolley delayed by shark

An ACTA trolley was delayed this afternoon when it struck a six-foot frozen shark that had apparently fallen onto the track in the vicinity of Iger Square, according to ACTA and police officials.

The shark had apparently been hung by a rope from electrical piping above the trolley tracks. The rope broke and the shark fell onto the tracks below, an ACTA official theorized.

The trolley was heading toward Museum Row on the ACTA's Central Line when it encountered the shark between Celardo and Elias streets about 2:40 p.m., officials said.

The shark had become wedged between the wheels of the trolley, but caused neither derailment nor injuries. The accident did, however, cause "minimal" delay in service, said an ACTA official.

Origin of the frozen and gutted shark was not immediately known. No sharks had been reported missing, according to a spokesman for the Astro City Aquarium.

YOU ARE NOW LEAVING
ASTRO CITY
PLEASE DRIVE CAREFULLY

CHAPTER 3

'COURSE, IT DON'T ALWAYS EXACTLY GO *RIGHT*.

BUT I DON'T THINK THE COPS EVEN *SAW* ME. THEY WERE TOO BUSY COLLARIN' *JIMMY* AN' THE *OTHERS*.

AWRIGHT, *AWRIGHT*, SO I *SCREWED UP*. I WAS THE LOOKOUT, AND I SHOULDA BEEN *LOOKIN' OUT* BETTER.

BUT IT AIN'T *ALL* MY FAULT.

IF THEY HADN'T MISSED A *SILENT ALARM* OR SOMETHIN', THERE WOULDN'T'VE *BEEN* COPS TO GET PAST ME!

ONE FOULED-UP *WAREHOUSE* HEIST AIN'T NOTHIN' SPECIAL. IT'S WHAT HAPPENS *AFTER*.

NOT MUCH TO SEE HERE MOST NIGHTS. JUST A BUNCHA YUPPIES AFRAID OF THE *DARK*.

I'D RUN ALL THE WAY TO THE EDGE OF *THE SHOP* --

-- WHERE THE WAREHOUSES AN' BODEGAS SMACK INTO RESTORED *BROWNSTONES* AN' *FERN BARS*.

AN' THAT *AIN'T* THE STORY ANYWAYS.

BUT LIKE I SAY --

HALF THE GUYS ON BIRO ISLAND GOT JUGGED BY JACK-IN-THE-BOX ONE TIME OR ANOTHER. AN' HALF THE GUYS WALKIN' LOOSE --

-- THEY KNOW WHAT IT'S LIKE TO GET *CONFETTIED* -- OR TO BE ZAPPED STUPID BY ONE A' THOSE FREAKY *RUBBER NOSES* A' HIS.

THAT'S THE *TRICK*, AIN'T IT? YOU GOTTA KEEP YOUR *EYES* OPEN --

-- YOU GOTTA LOOK FOR YOUR *OPPORTUNITIES* --

-- BUT *STILL* --

-- THIS IS A *GREAT* TOWN.

CRAIG AVENUE BAR & GRILL

CRAIG AVENUE BAR & GRILL

THURSDAY NIGHT, EVERETT PIER. A *BILL* A MAN.

THAT'S A *TWO-BILL* JOB -- !

JUST *LIFTIN'* AN' *LOADIN'*, EYES. ONE BILL, TAKE IT OR *LEAVE* IT.

THE *CRAIG AVENUE* AIN'T IN THEM TOURIST GUIDES EITHER -- IT'S STRICTLY A *NEIGHBORHOOD* PLACE. A GOOD PLACE TO *TALK* --

YEAH, YEAH. TELL 'EM I'M *IN*, JOHNNY.

THE *CONFESSOR* CAUGHT GLEASON *UPTOWN.*

-- MAYBE PICK UP SOME *WORK.* AN' MAYBE I WAS SITTIN' ON A *GOLDMINE* --

HEY, *EYES!* I HEAR JIMMY WENT DOWN LAST NIGHT -- ON *YOUR* LOOKOUT.

SAW *WINGED VICTORY*

LOVE TO GET *CAUGHT* BY HER

BOILERMAKER! HA -- BOILERMAKER OUGHTTA FIGHT *THE CONFESSOR!*

THAT AIN'T *FAIR*, LEV. *JACK-IN-THE-BOX* -- HE WAS *WAITIN'* FOR US.

GAGGED ME, THEN IN CAME THE *COPS.* I BARELY MANAGED TO *SLIP AWAY.*

YOU? SNUCK OUT ON *JACK-IN-THE-BOX?*

PULL THE *OTHER* ONE, EYES!

GO AHEAD, *SCOFF! DON'T* BELIEVE ME!

IT AIN'T LIKE I'M GONNA HAVE TO PUT UP WITH *ANY A'* THIS MUCH LONGER...

YOU *GOT* SOMETHIN', EYES?

YOU ONTO SOMETHIN' WITH *MONEY* IN IT?

ANYTHING IN IT FOR YOUR *BUDDIES?*

I WAS PLANNIN' TO GET THE GUYS TO HELP ME FIGGER OUT HOW TO SELL JACK'S I.D. TO *THE DEACON* --

UH --

-- BUT THAT WON'T *PLAY* --

-- THEY'D CUT ME *OUT* OF THE DEAL AS SOON AS THEY GOT THE *CHANCE.*

I CAN SEE IT *NOW* --

GUYS...

GUYS...

OH, LOOK -- IT'S A *RUFFIAN* OF SOME SORT!

HE TRIED TO TOUCH MY *NEW SUIT!*

I'LL HAVE THE CHAUFFEUR *ROUGH HIM UP* AND TOSS HIM INTO THE RIVER. SUCH *IMPERTINENCE.*

IT'S NOT LIKE I WOULDN'T DO THE SAME *MYSELF.*

UH, IT'S *NOTHIN',* GUYS. I GOT AN OFFER TO DO SOME WORK ON MY *AUNT'S HOUSE,* OUT IN CALIFORNIA. I'M THINKIN' ABOUT IT. LIKE A *VACATION,* Y'KNOW?

YEAH, RIGHT. LIKE A *VACATION.*

UH - HUH.

WORKIN' ON HER *HOUSE.*

GUYS, *HONEST* -- IT AIN'T --

74

I GOTTA **GET** OUT -- !

MEN

SPRONG

THKASH

KRATT

-GUHH-

-MMF-

THE **MIDDLEMAN'S** PICKING UP SOME STOLEN GOODS THURSDAY NIGHT, I HEAR.

I WANT TO KNOW **WHAT** --

-- I WANT TO KNOW **WHERE** --

KRAK

"-- AND I WANT TO KNOW **NOW!**"

THIS IS **BAD**. WORST THING YOU CAN DO IN THIS TOWN IS DRAW **ATTENTION** TO YOURSELF. DOUBLE WORST IS **MASKED** ATTENTION.

THE **GUYS** KNOW I'VE GOT SOMETHIN' -- MAYBE **JACK-IN-THE-BOX** KNOWS --

-- I COULD BE IN REAL **TROUBLE** HERE --

-- AND I DON'T EVEN **GOT** NOTHIN' FOR **SURE** YET. GOTTA CHECK THINGS OUT.

I **FIGGER** IF HE WAS CHANGIN' CLOTHES IN THAT ALLEY, HE **LIVES** OR **WORKS** AROUND HERE --

-- SO IF I STAKE OUT THE PLACE LONG ENOUGH, I'LL **SEE** HIM AGAIN.

DAMN **YUPPIES**.

TAKE OVER A NEIGHBORHOOD -- DRAIN ALL THE **CHARACTER** OUTTA IT --

-- LIKE **VAMPIRES** OR SOMETHIN'.

INGELS STREET -- IT DIDN'T USED TO BE A **NICE** PLACE, BUT AT LEAST IT WAS A **PLACE** --

-- NOT THIS URBAN-RENEWED UPSCALE CAPPUCCINO **NOTHING**.

DAVIS GROCERS USED TO BE OVER **THERE**, AND KAMEN'S DELI --

-- ELDER'S GYM WAS RIGHT AROUND -- *HEY!*

THAT'S *HIM!* AN' THE WOMAN WITH HIM -- I *SEEN* HER!

SHE DOES THE MORNING NEWS ON *CHANNEL 3!*

I COULD WAIT 'TIL THEY'RE *GONE* -- GET THE NAME OFF THE *BUZZER* --

-- BUT A LOTTA PEOPLE DON'T LABEL THEIR BUZZERS, AND --

'SCUSE ME -- UH -- COULD I HAVE AN *AUTOGRAPH?*

SURE -- WHO SHOULD I SIGN IT *TO?*

UH, UM -- *JACK. JACK... BACHSINGER.*

THERE YOU GO, MISTER BACHSINGER.

THANKS.

NO, THANK *YOU* -- JUST KEEP WATCHING THE SHOW!

THAT WAS *STUPID! STUPID! BACHSINGER* -- WHY DIDN'T I JUST SAY *"JACK INNABOX"* AND SLIT MY THROAT RIGHT IN *FRONT* OF 'EM?!

OH, *MAN,* I'M IN *TROUBLE...*

I FIND HER IN THE ROCKET'S *METRO* SECTION A YEAR BACK -- *TAMRA DIXON.*

BUT -- *DOES* HE GOT *ME?*

EVEN IF HE *HADN'T* SEEN ME -- JACK *BACHSINGER?*

GEEZ, I CAN SEE IT *NOW* --

SHE'S ATTENDING SOME *CHARITY* THING WITH HER HUSBAND -- *ZACHARY JOHNSON,* "OWNER AND CEO OF THE SMALL-BUT GROWING Z.J. TOYS."

I GOT HIM.

EYES -- OH, *EYES* -- !

SOME PEOPLE SEE *TOO MUCH,* EYES -- !

KA-PLINK KA-PLINK KA-

79

WORD IS, SAMARITAN BUSTED UP SOME *PYRAMID* BASE IN *TURKEY*, AN' ALL THEIR WEAPONS AN' STUFF GOT *CONFISCATED.* BUT THEY KIND OF *"FELL OFF A TRUCK"* --

-- AN' THAT'S HOW THE *MIDDLEMAN* GOT 'EM. HE NEVER *ADMITS* ANYTHING LIKE THAT --

-- I THINK HE *FIGGERS* HE'LL HAVE TO *PAY* US MORE IF WE KNOW IT'S IMPORTANT --

=UFF=

-- BUT THAT'S HOW HE GETS *MOST* OF HIS STUFF.

STILL, HE HAD TO PAY US EXTRA TONIGHT *ANYWAY.*

NOT ENOUGH GUYS *SHOWED UP*, FOR SOME REASON, AN' US THAT DID WOULDA *WALKED* IF HE WASN'T PAYIN' EXTRA FOR THE EXTRA LUGGIN'.

FASTER! FASTER!

I WONDER WHY NOBODY MUCH *SHOWED UP?* THE WORK'S A *PAIN*, BUT THE MONEY SPENDS JUST AS GOOD AS ANY OTHER --

THE TRUCKS ARE *RENTALS!* WE'VE GOT TO BE DONE AND GONE IN --

-- AN' IT'S NOT LIKE THERE'S A *BOXIN' MATCH* ON OR ANY --

THKASSH

THKASSH

HUH?!

=GHUH!=

=MMF=

SPROING THKASSH

WARNING
DANGEROUS CARGO
NO VISITORS
NO SMOKING
NO OPEN LIGHTS

-- BUT I *MADE* IT!

IF I GET TO THE *DEACON* -- SELL HIM THE *SECRET* --

-- MAYBE HE CAN *PROTECT* ME --

-- HE'LL *HIDE* ME --

-- I CAN *SEE* IT --

WHATDDYA *WANT,* PUTZ?

I GOTTA -- I GOTTA SEE THE *DEACON* --

DEACON DON'T *SEE* LOWLIFES. WHAT'S YOUR *BIZNIS?*

I KNOW -- KNOW JACK-IN-THE-BOX'S *SECRET IDENTITY* --

HM?

YEAH, THE DEACON'D WANT T'KNOW *THAT* AWRIGHT. SO I TELL YOU *WHAT* --

-- YOU TELL ME THE GUY'S *NAME* --

CRRNK

-- AN' *I'LL* TELL THE DEACON -- !

85

I WAS GONNA MAKE A *MILLION BUCKS* -- GONNA BE *RICH* --

-- BUT --

COULD I GO TO THE *NEWS*, EXPOSE THE SECRET -- WOULD *THAT* GET JACK OFF MY BACK?

LIKE HIS *WIFE* WOULDN'T KNOW. WOULDN'T TELL HIM.

MAYBE THE *PAPERS*? NEWSPAPERMEN DON'T REVEAL THEIR SOURCES --

-- EXCEPT THE *DEACON* WOULD WANT TO KNOW, AND I BET THEY REVEAL 'EM WHEN YOU START CUTTIN' OFF *BODY PARTS* --

DAMMIT, *DAMMIT*...

I CAN REMEMBER THE *FIRST TIME* I SAW JACK-IN-THE-BOX --

-- IT WAS SUCH A *THRILL* --

MOMMY! LOOKIT THE *MAN*!

YES, DEAR. HE'S *HELPING* US ALL -- HE'S A *FRIEND*.

WOW! THIS IS THE *BEST* PLACE --

"-- I DON'T WANNA *EVER* LIVE *ANYWHERE ELSE!*"

AAAAH!

IT'S *HIM!*

IT'S --

THIS IS GONNA *KILL* ME. IT WASN'T EVEN *HIM,* AND IT ALMOST KILLED ME.

I CAN'T EVEN GO BACK TO MY *ROOM* -- HE MIGHT BE *WAITIN'* --

OR MAYBE --

-- MAYBE HE DOESN'T EVEN *KNOW.*

MAYBE HE LOOKED AT ME FUNNY ON THE STREET 'CAUSE HE'D SEEN ME AT THE *CRAIG AVENUE* BUT COULDN'T PLACE ME.

MAYBE HE WAS AFTER THE *MIDDLEMAN* TONIGHT.

MAYBE I'M *SAFE.*

MAYBE I'M *SAFE* FROM HIM -- FROM THE *DEACON* --

-- FROM THE GUYS AT THE *CRAIG* --

-- THE *PAPERS* --

-- *MAYBE* --

-- *MAYBE* --

TICKETS

AN' THAT'S WHAT *HAPPENED.*

I RISKED GOIN' BACK TO MY ROOM. THERE WASN'T NOBODY THERE, BUT I JUMPED AT EVERY SHADOW.

I GOT SOME CLOTHES, MY TOOTHBRUSH, MY *EMERGENCY STASH.*

IT'S A *BIG COUNTRY,* AND THIS IS JUST *ONE TOWN.*

THERE'S OPPORTUNITY *ANYWHERE* FOR A MAN WHO KEEPS HIS EYES OPEN --

-- FOR A *SHARP-EYED* MAN WHO --

SHFF

-- NO.

ON THE *OTHER HAND* --

RUS TERMI

VMMMMMM

-- MAYBE *NOT.*

ANCHORAGE

YOU ARE NOW LEAVING **ASTRO CITY** PLEASE DRIVE CAREFULLY

C H A P T E R

MORNING IN *SHADOW HILL*, BELOW THE LOOMING BULK OF MOUNT KIRBY'S EASTERN FACE -- SHADOW HILL, WHERE NIGHT FALLS *FIRST* IN ASTRO CITY.

BUT *MORNING* COMES TO US AS IT DOES TO *ANYONE.*

I TALK WITH MAMA AS I CHECK THE *WOLFSBANE* IN THE WINDOW CATCHES, FRESHENING IT WHERE NEEDED.

I TAP MY *CRUCIFIX*, TO REASSURE MYSELF THAT IT'S THERE. I KISS MAMA AND WISH A GOOD DAY FOR HER.

I SAY THE WORDS AND OPEN THE DOOR -- A GOOD *OAK* DOOR, WITH ASH IN THE FRAME, AND THE SIGN OF *TEUSZ* IN BRASS.

THE AIR SMELLS LIKE *LIFE*, AND LIKE SOMETHING WAKING UP.

I WALK ALONG OUR *COBBLED STREETS*, AS *SHUTTERS* ARE THROWN OPEN TO THE SUN AND THE *BUSTLE* OF THE DAY BEGINS.

THE LESSER *NIGHT CREATURES* STILL CROUCH IN THE SHRINKING SHADOWS, MUTTERING AND SNARLING SOFTLY.

I PAY THEM *NO MIND.* GUARDED AS I AM, THEY CANNOT *APPROACH* ME, AND IN MINUTES --

-- THEY'LL HAVE RETREATED *FULLY* BEFORE THE SUN.

THE *HANGED MAN* MAKES THE LAST OF HIS NIGHTLY ROUNDS. I *NOD* TO HIM, AS ALWAYS, OFFERING THANKS FOR HIS PROTECTIVE *VIGIL*.

AS ALWAYS, HE MAKES NO SIGN OF ACKNOWLEDGEMENT.

GRANDENETTI AVE

KIEFER ST

ONE WAY

ONE WAY

I BUY MY BREAKFAST AT *GROZA'S* -- A BIALY AND THE THICK, SWEET COFFEE THEY DON'T MAKE DOWNTOWN.

ONE WAY

BUS STOP

AND THEN THE *BUS* IS HERE, AS PUNCTUAL AS EVER, DRAWING ITS *DAILY PATTERN* THROUGH THE WINDING STREETS.

CITY CENTER

I AM *ALONE*, AS ALWAYS. NOT MANY OF US LEAVE THE HILL EACH DAY.

MORNING, MARTA.

GOOD MORNING, MISTER IRONS.

I *SWEAR* --

-- I DON'T KNOW *HOW* YOU DO IT. I COULDN'T *LIVE* UP HERE -- GIVES ME THE WILLIES JUST DRIVING *THROUGH* THE PLACE.

ZENIC'S Market

AND THAT, TOO, IS A PART OF THE *MORNING*. PART OF WHAT I HAVE COME TO THINK OF AS THE RITUAL OF *CHANGE*.

MISTER IRONS'S SIGH OF RELIEF IS A SIGNAL THAT WE HAVE *LEFT* THE HILL --

-- LEFT THE WORLD WHERE I AM MY PARENTS' CHILD, A DAUGHTER OF MY CULTURE AND A FOLLOWER OF THE *OLD RULES* --

92

WE TRAVEL THROUGH THE *OTHER NEIGHBORHOODS,* ON DOWN THE HILL --

-- FASS GARDENS, RENSIE AVENUE, DERBYFIELD --

-- AND SOME OF THE PASSENGERS *GLANCE* AT THE GIRL FROM SHADOW HILL, LOOK AWAY AND SIT *SOMEWHERE ELSE* --

-- AND THEIR *MORNING CHATTER* FILLS THE BUS --

RENTING A NEW *PLACE*

GOOD *WEEKEND,* AND YOU?

HEAR *DEMOLITIA* BROKE OUT OF JAIL

REBUILT HER COMMODE AND PRISON COT INTO A *JACKHAMMER,* AND

FIRST FAMILY TRYING TO *CATCH* HER BEFORE SHE FREES THE REST OF THE *UNHOLY ALLIANCE*

LOOK!

USED CAR, BUT I'M GOING TO WORK ON IT

KIDS RAN ME *RAGGED*

IT'S *WINGED VICTORY.*

THE NEWS SAID SHE BROKE UP AN *ARMORED-CAR HIJACKING* LAST NIGHT.

THE SIGHT OF HER, PROUD AND NOBLE, NEVER FAILS TO SET MY HEART RACING. THE WAY SHE SETS HER OWN COURSE, FREE OF *GRAVITY,* OF *RULES* --

-- THE WAY SHE DOES WHAT SHE THINKS IS *RIGHT,* WITHOUT A CARE FOR TRADITION, OR THE APPROVAL OF OTHERS --

-- SHE MAKES ME FEEL LIKE I CAN DO *ANYTHING.*

LOVELY, JUST *LOVELY.*

TROUBLE, IF YOU ASK ME

CAMPS OF HERS -- INDOCTRINATING *CHILDREN*

NOTHING BUT A *CULT LEADER*

DANGEROUS

HONESTLY! WOULD YOU *LISTEN* TO YOURSELVES? WINGED VICTORY'S JUST CAPTURED SOME *CRIMINALS --*

-- AND THIS IS THE *THANKS* SHE GETS? MUTTERINGS AND *SLANDERS?*

I SHUDDER TO THINK WHAT WE'D DO *WITHOUT* THEM -- WITHOUT *ALL* OF THEM!

THE OTHERS FALL *SILENT* AT THAT, AS WELL THEY *SHOULD --*

-- AND WE TRAVEL ON UNTIL WE REACH *BINDERBECK PLAZA,* WHERE MOST OF US WORK.

I HAVE ALWAYS *LIKED* BINDERBECK PLAZA --

-- IT WAS ONCE THE *DUTCH* SECTION OF TOWN, BUT GREW AND CHANGED TO BECOME THE *HEART OF THE CITY --*

-- JUST AS, BY THIS TIME, THE GIRL FROM SHADOW HILL IS *NO MORE --*

-- REPLACED BY AN *INDEPENDENT* YOUNG WOMAN -- A PART OF THE *ENERGY* AND *SPIRIT* THAT GIVE THE CITY *LIFE.*

BUT PERHAPS I *OVER-ROMANTICIZE.*

I AM, AFTER ALL, MERELY A *JUNIOR CLERK* IN THE ACCOUNTING DEPARTMENT OF ONE OF THE CITY'S LARGER *LAW FIRMS* --

GRANT, MILLER, CONROY McCONNELL & INGERSOL

-- NOT LIKE *DARCY CONROY,* MY BOSS -- AND THE FIRM'S BRIGHTEST STAR.

WE'RE ROLLING!

BUT DON'T YOU WORRY ABOUT THE *DANGER,* MS. CONROY? AFTER ALL --

SHE'S A CELEBRITY -- THE FIANCEE OF *NICK FURST,* OF THE *FIRST FAMILY.* I ENVY HER *POISE* IN THE PUBLIC SPOTLIGHT --

-- THE WAY SHE WALKS THROUGH THE WORLD LIKE IT *BELONGS* TO HER.

-- ALL THE FIRST FAMILY'S ENEMIES KNOW WHERE TO *FIND* YOU...

I DON'T WORRY ABOUT *THAT,* STEVE -- I'M NOT THE TYPE TO *HIDE* FROM TROUBLE.

BESIDES, YOU SEE THIS *BROOCH?* NICKIE GAVE IT TO ME.

IT LOOKS LIKE IT'S JUST A *PIN,* BUT IF I TURN THE DESIGN IN THE FRAME LIKE --

-- WELL, I WON'T DO IT NOW, BUT IF I *DID,* IT WOULD SET OFF ALL KINDS OF ALARMS AT NICKIE'S HEAD-QUARTERS --

-- AND HE'D KNOW TO *COME A'RUNNING.*

SHE *SPOKE* TO ME, ONCE. *SMILED* AT ME.

HEY, MARTA -- I THINK THE CAMERAS *CAUGHT* YOU!

YOU GONNA BE TAPING THE *NEWS* TONIGHT?

IT'S *CHANNEL 4*, BILLY -- WE DON'T *GET* IT UP ON THE HILL.

Please rinse spoons and put in drainer

Last cup? Make more!

WILL YOU *LISTEN* TO HER?!

I'LL TELL YOU FOR NOTHIN', I COULDN'T DO WHAT *YOU* DO, MARTA! LIVIN' UP THERE ON *SHADOW HILL* --

-- DON'T YOU HAVE, LIKE, *VAMPIRES* UP THERE?

SOME. THEY'RE NOT AS BAD AS YOU *THINK*, THOUGH.

I GREW UP THERE. I GUESS I'M JUST *USED* TO IT.

"NOT AS BAD AS YOU *THINK!*" *LISTEN* TO HER!

I SMILE, AND GO ABOUT MY WORK --

-- BUT SHELLIE'S COMMENTS *STAY* WITH ME. EVEN *HERE*, I'M STILL A GIRL FROM THE *HILL*.

I WONDER WHAT THEY'D THINK IF I TOLD THEM MY *MORNING ROUTINE?* IT'S SO *NORMAL* TO ME, AND YET --

MARTA?

HI, JENNY -- WHAT'S UP?

19 NOVEMBER 95

LOOK, MARTA -- I WAS *WONDERING* --

-- ONE OF THE GALS IN MY APARTMENT JUST TOOK A JOB IN *SAN FRANCISCO*, SO WE'RE LOOKING FOR A NEW *ROOMIE* --

"-- IF YOU'RE INTERESTED."

NO. DEFINITE NOT!

BUT MAMA, I --

THIS IS WHAT COMES! I TOLD YOU, NICU!

WE SPEAK ENGLISH IN THE HOUSE SO SHE GROWS UP NOT BEING AN OUTSIDER! AND WHAT HAPPENS?

SHE BECOMES ONE OF THEM! SHE WORKS DOWN THERE, NOW SHE LIVES DOWN THERE --

MAMA --

-- DOES SHE MARRY DOWN THERE, AND THEN WE NEVER SEE HER AGAIN?!

GHEORGHI VASILIU, HE NEEDS HELP AT HIS SHOP.

THIS IS TRUE, MARTA! VASILIU NEEDS A PERSON TO KEEP BOOKS -- AND HIS BUTCHER SHOP MAKES PLENTY MONEY!

WHAT DOES --

YOU ARE GOOD WITH NUMBERS --

-- AND VASILIU, HE'S SINGLE AND NOT BAD-LOOKING --

MAMA!

I CAN'T BLAME THEM EITHER, I SUPPOSE. THE HILL IS THEIR WORLD --

DOWNTOWN IS AS ALIEN TO THEM AS THOUGHTS OF WOLFSBANE ARE TO SHELLIE IN THE OFFICE. AND IT'S NOT THAT I DON'T LIKE IT HERE --

-- THIS IS MY HOME. THE CROOKED, WINDING STREETS -- THE SMELL OF GARLIC AND OF BREAD BAKING -- GRANDMAMA'S GRAVE --

98

-- OF COURSE, I WOULDN'T MIND *AT ALL* HAVING MORE THAN TWO T.V. STATIONS, AND ONLY *ONE* OF THEM MOSTLY CLEAR --

--ILLION-DOLLAR REFURBISHMENT OF OUR *MOST FAMOUS* LANDMARK!

AS ALL ASTRO CITIZENS KNOW, OUR *GLEAMING SILVER* SYMBOL IS *MORE THAN* AN ORNAMENT --

-- MORE THAN A MEMORIAL TO A HERO WHO GAVE HIS LIFE TO *SAVE MILLIONS* --

WE'RE NOT TRULY SO *DIFFERENT*, ARE WE?

FILE FOOTAGE

WOLFSBANE, CRUCIFIXES, SIGNAL-BROOCHES, EMERGENCY BEACONS. THEY HAVE *THEIR* TALISMANS, AND WE HAVE *OURS* --

-- WE JUST *SHAPE* THEM DIFFERENTLY, THAT'S ALL.

-- *BUT* A *BEACON* IN TIMES OF *EMERGENCY* --

-- ALERTING ASTRO CITY'S *SUPERHUMAN* CHAMPIONS TO ANY DANGER THAT THREATENS *INNOCENTS* --

-- THE *COLOR* AND *PATTERN* OF THE RINGS TELL OUR HEROES THE *LOCATION* OF THE DANGER, AND CERTAIN OTHER --

THAT'S NOT SO *STRANGE.* ANYWHERE YOU GROW UP, YOU NEED TO KNOW HOW TO BE *SAFE.*

I REMEMBER *GRANDMAMA* TEACHING ME ABOUT THE PROTECTIVE PROPERTIES OF THE PLANTS IN HER *GARDEN* --

MISTLETOE, CHILD. WILL PROTECT YOU FROM THE *PRINCE OF DARKNESS,* FOR HE NOT STAND ITS PURITY.

ALSO, GOOD IF NEED TO SPEAK TO *GHOSTS,* BUT THAT FOR LATER.

-- MAKING SURE I KNEW HOW TO *TAKE CARE* OF MYSELF --

HE *LOOKS* AT ME!

I CAN'T SEE PAST THE RAGGED EDGES OF *BURLAP* THAT HIDE HIS EYES, BUT THERE'S SOMETHING IN THOSE *DARK SMEARS* --

-- AND I KNOW IT'S A *WARNING* --

I RACK MY BRAIN, BUT I'VE DONE *EVERYTHING* --

-- BUT A WARNING OF *WHAT?*

MARTA?

MORNING, MARTA.

-- THE LATCH CAUGHT, THE WINDOWS ARE SAFE, THE HEARTH DOESN'T NEED RE-BLESSING FOR ANOTHER MONTH --

JAZZ FESTIVAL NOV 10 THRU NOV 19 ...PITORIUM

-- I OWE, I OWE, SO OFF TO WORK --

-- SPRANG *FLAMETHROWER* FROM LEAVENWORTH LAST NIGHT -- THAT'S THE *ENTIRE* UNHOLY ALLIANCE --

-- HONOR GUARD'S *ON THEIR* BUTTS -- CAUGHT UP WITH THEM IN THE *QUAD CITIES* --

-- *CASH MONEY* SAMARITAN'LL HAVE 'EM LOCKED UP BY --

AND I THINK OF MY *DREAM*, AND THE CRACKING STREETS, THE CLUTCHING *SHADOWS* --

-- AND I DON'T WANT TO BE A SCARED LITTLE GIRL ANY MORE, BUT I CAN FEEL THE BULK OF THE *HILL WEIGHING DOWN* ON ME, BURYING ME *ALIVE* --

RRMBLL

THIS WAY!

STAIRS

INTO THE *STAIRWELL!* IT'S REINFORCED -- AND WE'VE GOT TO GET TO *GROUND* LEVEL!

THE *ELEVATORS* --

FORGET THE ELEVATORS! THEY'RE NOT *SAFE!*

HELLO? HELLO, *POLICE?!*

MS. CONROY CUTS THROUGH OUR PANIC -- SOUNDING SO *CONFIDENT,* SO *SURE* OF HERSELF, THAT WE OBEY WITHOUT THINKING.

-- I'VE GOT A LINE THEY *CAN'T* CUT!

LINE'S *DEAD* -- THEY MUST'VE *CUT* IT -- !

DON'T *WORRY* ABOUT IT, JENNY. JUST GET DOWN THOSE *STAIRS* --

COME ON, NICKIE. *PHONE'S* RINGING -- !

DLEET
DLEET
DLEET
DLEET
DLEET
DLEET
DLEET

SURELY SHE KNOWS THE *WAY OUT* --

-- SHE KNOWS THE *RULES.*

WE NEVER *DID* FIND OUT WHY THEY ATTACKED.

IT MIGHT HAVE BEEN DEMOLITIA GOING AFTER *MS. CONROY,* WHO'D BEEN THE D.A. WHO FIRST PUT HER IN JAIL, YEARS BACK.

FLAMETHROWER! OVER *THERE!*

GOT 'EM!

GLOWWORM BLAMED THE CITY FOR THE ACCIDENT THAT *TRANSFORMED* HIM --

BUT ALL ACROSS THE *PLAZA,* PEOPLE FLOOD INTO STAIRWELLS OR HUDDLE IN CLOSETS, WEEPING AND PRAYING --

-- AND THE WORLD KEEPS *SHAKING* --

FRA KAMM

AH -- !

IT'S *BLOCKED!* CROSS OVER TO THE *OTHER* STAIRWELL!

KEEP *MOVING* -- DON'T SLO DOWN!

106

AND IF *HE* WAS A REAL PERSON, THEN THE OTHERS...

CRITICAL CA TRANSPORT

SOMETHING *CHANGED* FOR ME THAT DAY, WATCHING THE AFTERMATH -- *RESCUE WORKERS* DOING THEIR JOBS, *T.V. NEWS CREWS* EVERYWHERE --

CITY CENTER -- IT'S JUST A *PLACE.* A DIFFERENT KIND OF PLACE FROM SHADOW HILL, BUT NOT *THAT* DIFFERENT.

THERE ARE *HEROES* AND *MONSTERS* IN BOTH PLACES. AND DOWN HERE --

MARTA?

-- THERE ARE *RULES* DOWN HERE, TOO.

MS. CONROY!

IF YOU DON'T WANT TO GO *HOME* TONIGHT -- IF YOU'RE SCARED BECAUSE FLAMETHROWER'S STILL ON THE *LOOSE* --

-- I CAN PUT YOU UP AT *MY* PLACE.

MS. CONROY IS A *GOOD* PERSON. KIND, AND SMART, AND *BRAVE.*

BUT SHE'S NOT *MAGIC* -- SHE JUST KNOWS THE RULES. SHE HAS HER TALISMAN, AND IT *WORKS* FOR HER.

I'LL BE *ALL RIGHT,* MS. CONROY. NOBODY WOULD COME UP TO SHADOW HILL AT *NIGHT* --

-- NOT IF THEY DON'T KNOW HOW TO *TAKE CARE* OF THEMSELVES.

BUT IT'S *HER* TALISMAN. THAT'S THE *REAL* DIFFERENCE.

I'M *SAFE* HERE. THERE ARE UNTHINKABLE *DANGERS* SWIRLING IN THE SHADOWS OUTSIDE MY WINDOW, BUT THEY'RE MY *PROTECTION.*

THEY'RE MY SHIELD AGAINST THE DANGERS I *DON'T* UNDERSTAND.

I SIT AND THINK ABOUT *CHARMS* AND *TALISMANS.* MS. *CONROY* HAS A TALISMAN. THE *CITY* HAS A TALISMAN.

WHAT DO *I* HAVE?

I WAS SO *SCARED.* I WANTED TO BE *ANYWHERE* BUT HERE -- I WANTED TO GET *OUT,* TO GO -- TO BE *SOMEWHERE ELSE.*

AND I SIT, AND I WATCH THE SHAPES IN THE MIST, AND I *WONDER.*

WAS IT REALLY THE *HILL* THAT SCARED ME?

I SIT UP ALL NIGHT, AND IN THE MORNING I CALL THE OFFICE. THEY'VE RENTED *TEMPORARY SPACE,* BUT I CAN TAKE A FEW DAYS OFF, THEY SAY.

I DON'T *NEED* TO.

I CHECK THE *WINDOW-LATCHES.* I UNSEAL THE *DOOR.* I TAP MY *CRUCIFIX.*

I BUY MY BIALY AND COFFEE AT *GROZA'S.* I NOD TO THE HANGED MAN.

I BREATHE IN THE *SOFT MORNING AIR,* AND I EAT MY BREAKFAST IN THE WARM LIGHT OF THE *SUN.*

PERHAPS I CAN FIND AN *APARTMENT* TO RENT NEARBY. I'LL HAVE TO ASK AROUND.

YOU ARE NOW LEAVING **ASTRO CITY** PLEASE DRIVE CAREFULLY

CHAPTER 5

Once upon a time...

...there was a little old man who lived in an undistinguished rooming house on the **north** side of Astro City.

If you asked him, the little old man would say that he worked **forty-five years** as a draftsman in a basement room without windows, and he intended to spend his retirement out-of-doors as much as **possible**, breathing the air, looking at the sun and sky until he finally managed to flush the fluorescent light from his system.

But the little old man was a liar.

There was no basement room. There was no fluorescent light.

And he did not walk outside to look at the sun.

RECONNAISSANCE

I WALK FOR AN *HOUR AND A HALF* WITHOUT SEEING ANYTHING ELSE.

I BUY *THREE NEWSPAPERS* AND A *CURRENT* COVERING THE *STARWOMAN RETROSPECTIVE* AT THE MUSEUM OF MODERN HISTORY.

ASTRO CITY ROCKET

CLEOPATRA VS **GNOMICRON**

WH--

HUH?

HEY --

HEY, THAT WAS --

SAMARITAN. TRAVELING SLOWER THAN USUAL SPEED, FROM THE *LOOK* OF IT.

OFF TO STOP ANOTHER *DISASTER,* NO DOUBT. OR TO SAVE LIVES IN SOME *OTHER* WAY.

WHATEVER IT IS, IT WILL PROBABLY BE ON THE *RADIO NEWS* WITHIN THE HOUR.

I REST MY *LEGS* IN THE PARK.

TIME TO UPDATE MY *FILES.*

EL ROBO

STATUS: Active
BIRTH NAME: Manuel de la Cruz
CAPSULE: Human/Machinery hybrid. Onboard arsenal [see expanded description for partial list]
AFFILIATION: Astro City Irregulars [not known to operate solo]

BASE OF OPERATIONS: Astro City
RANGE OF OPERATIONS: International [with team]
UPDATE: Vulnerable to magnetic fields

STARWOMAN

STATUS: Inactive [this star system]
BIRTH NAME: Pr'slla of K'ntar

CAPSULE: K'ntar royal family, standard energy-manipulation abilities
AFFILIATION: Honor Guard [former]
BASE OF OPERATIONS: K'ntar
RANGE OF OPERATIONS: Global w/interstellar transport abilities
UPDATE: Contact matrix in Astro City Museum of Modern History, potentially functional

SAMARITAN

STATUS: Active
BIRTH NAME: Unknown

CAPSULE: Apparently enhanced human. Vast physical, energy powers [see expanded description]
AFFILIATION: Honor Guard
BASE OF OPERATIONS: Astro City
RANGE OF OPERATIONS: Global [solo] Global [w/team]
UPDATE: Potentially distractible [see behavioral pattern analysis]

TAKATAKATAKATAKATAKATAKATAKATAKATAKAT

GNOMICRON

STATUS: Destroyed

BIRTH NAME: Inapplicable
CAPSULE: Mechanical Warrior
(powered by mystic furnace)
AFFILIATION: Mountain gnomes
BASE OF OPERATIONS:
Glittertinden, Norway
RANGE OF OPERATIONS:
International (limited to
mountain areas)
UPDATE: No longer destroyed;
disabled and imprisoned

QUARREL II

STATUS: Active
BIRTH NAME:
Jessica Darlene
Taggart

CAPSULE: Sharpshooter w/specialized
projectile launcher (see expanded
description for projectile list); skilled
athlete but no extra-human abilities
AFFILIATION: Honor Guard, personal
connections to Street Angel (poss.
defunct), Crackerjack
BASE OF OPERATIONS: Astro City
RANGE OF OPERATIONS: International
? (solo), Global (w/ team)
UPDATE: Add to projectile list: Acid
quarrels, anesthetic-injection
("knockout") quarrels

CONFESSOR

STATUS: Active
BIRTH NAME: Unknown

NO KNOWN
PHOTOGRAPHS

CAPSULE: Crimefighter, abilities
not known
AFFILIATION: None known
BASE OF OPERATIONS: Astro City
RANGE OF OPERATIONS:
Astro City (w/rare exceptions)
UPDATE: Pattern of sightings
concentrated in area of
Grandenetti Cathedr___

AKATAKATAKATAKATAKATAKA

HEY,
WHASSUP?!

IZZAT THE NEW **720?** MAN, I **READ** ABOUT THOSE!

SWEET **MACHINE**, MAN! CAN I --

DON'T TOUCH IT!

IT IS **NOT** YOUR PRECIOUS 720, AND WHAT IT **IS** IS NONE OF YOUR **CONCERN!**

NOW BE **OFF** WITH YOU!

GEEZ! OVER**REACT** MUCH?!

I CAN FINISH THE **UPDATING** LATER. THE **NERVE** OF THE CHILD -- !

AS I WALK BACK TO MY **DWELLING,** ANGER **ROILS** WITHIN ME AT THE DISCOURTESY, AND I CONTEMPLATE SENDING THE SIGNAL **TONIGHT.**

BUT NO -- IT IS JUST THEIR **WAY.** THEIR POINT-LESS, CASUAL **FAMILIARITY.** I TAMP THE ANGER BACK --

-- RECAPTURING MY **COVER PERSONALITY** BY THE TIME I REACH MY DESTINATION.

HEY, MR. BRIDWELL -- LITTLE **COLD** OUT, ISN'T IT?

COLD AIR IS BETTER THAN **WALLS,** EUGENE. I AM CONTENT.

AND YOUR **AUDITION?** THAT WAS TODAY, YES?

YOU **DON'T MISS** A **THING,** MR. BRIDWELL. I STILL DON'T KNOW HOW THEY'RE GOING TO DO A MUSICAL OF "INHERIT THE WIND" --

-- ON MY PLANET, WOMEN ARE *WARRIORS* -- BOLD AND *STRONG*, WHOSE ACTIONS AND WORDS HAVE *WEIGHT* AND *FORCE*!

I, A MERE *MALE*, AM PRIVILEGED TO SERVE MY EMPIRE AS NOTHING BUT EYES IN THE SHADOWS -- BUT EVEN *I* MATTER!

IT WOULD ALMOST BE WORTH IT TO SEND THE *SIGNAL*, TO SET THE WHEELS OF INVASION IN *MOTION* --

-- SIMPLY TO *SEE* THOSE WOMEN DRAGGED SCREAMING TO THE WORK PITS TO TOIL THEMSELVES INTO THE *GRAVE*, THEIR TWITTERING SILENCED *FOREVER*!

BUT --

TRANSMISSION CONNECTION ESTABLISHED AWAITING SIGNAL.

BUT --

RECONNAISSANCE *CONTINUES*.

EXTENSIVE PARANORMAL ACTIVITY REQUIRES MORE TIME TO *CATALOGUE*. NO DETERMINATION *REACHED*.

TFK

-- WOULD SEEM TO *CONFIRM* THAT.

WHOAAA! HEY, NO KNOCKING THE HERO *OFF-BALANCE*, POPS --

IT WAS HIS OWN *WEIGHT* THAT MADE THE FLOOR GIVE WAY, BUT I DON'T CORRECT HIM.

-- *ESPECIALLY* WHEN HE'S SAVING YOUR LIFE!

HE REACTS QUITE *SMOOTHLY* AS HE AVOIDS FALLING WRECKAGE, TAKING US INTO THE *STAIRWELL* AND DOWN TO THE MAIN FLOOR.

I HAVE NEVER BEEN ABLE TO OBSERVE A *COSTUMED ADVENTURER* FROM QUITE THIS *VANTAGE POINT* --

-- AND I MUST *ADMIT* --

YOU KNOW, THE SERVICE IN HERE IS *TERRIBLE*. WHADDYA SAY, POPS --

KRASSH

-- HIS PHYSICAL SKILLS ARE QUITE *IMPRESSIVE*.

-- LET'S *BLOW* THIS POPSICLE STAND!

GOTTA GO!

HE MUST BE --

IT CAN'T BE!

THAT -- THAT *EUGENE* BOY -- !

ALWAYS SO *QUIET* --

THEY TWITTER AMONG *THEMSELVES*, REASSERTING ORDER IN THEIR MEANINGLESS LITTLE LIVES WITH EMPTY *WORDS* --

-- AND SUDDENLY I WANT A *RESOLUTION*.

I WANT TO *END* THIS, TO GET AWAY FROM THEIR CHATTER *FOREVER*.

SO EUGENE WALLACE IS *CRACKERJACK*. I NEVER *SUSPECTED*.

HE CLAIMS THAT ALL OTHERS PALE BESIDE HIM? VERY WELL -- I SHALL TAKE HIM AT HIS *WORD*.

WHILE HE RESCUED ME, I ATTACHED A *SENS-CIRCUIT* TO HIS BELT. IT WILL LET ME *SEE* AND *HEAR* WHATEVER HAPPENS TO HIM.

I SHALL OBSERVE HIM UNTIL *DAWN*, AND THEN I SHALL MAKE MY *FINAL JUDGMENT*.

NO MORE *DITHERING*. NO MORE *INDECISION*. EUGENE WALLACE SHALL BE HUMANITY IN *MICROCOSM* TONIGHT.

IF HE PROVES WORTHY, I SHALL *SPARE* HIS PLANET. IF NOT, WE ENSLAVE THIS WORLD AND ALL *ON* IT. BUT EITHER WAY --

JACK-IN-THE-BOX DEBUTED IN *1964* -- OR *1989*, IF ONE ASSUMES THAT THE CURRENT ONE IS A DIFFERENT MAN.

HE PREDATES CRACKERJACK BY EITHER *TWO* YEARS, OR *TWENTY-SEVEN*. IF ANYONE HAS CLAIM TO THE NAME, IT'S *HIM*.

SO THE WOMAN SAYS, "YOU IDIOT -- THIS IS A *DUCK*, NOT A *PIG!*" AND THE *BARTENDER* SAYS --

-- "I WAS *TALKING* TO THE *DUCK!*"

KRAK

WHAK

FINE, *DON'T* LAUGH! SEE IF *I* CARE!

KAMM

HERE YOU *GO*, OFFICERS --

-- A TRIO OF SLEEPING *NOT-SO-BEAUTIES*, COURTESY OF ASTRO CITY'S OWN *STAR ATTRACTION!*

REALLY? I DON'T SEE *SAMARITAN* AROUND *ANYWHERE...*

I DON'T SUPPOSE YOU'VE GOT ANY *EVIDENCE* ON THESE GUYS?

ANY INDICATION THEY WERE ACTUALLY DOING SOMETHING *CRIMINAL?*

AW, *PSHAW!* GOTTA LEAVE *SOMETHING* FOR YOU BOYS IN BLUE TO DO, RIGHT?

OTHERWISE, YOU'D HAVE TO CHANGE YOUR SLOGAN TO *"THEY ALSO SERVE WHO ONLY STAND AND WATCH!"*

TOODLES!

HI!

CRACKER-JACK! DO YOU *MIND?!* WE'RE ON *STAKEOUT* HERE!

THE *TECHSPERTS* ARE HITTING MUSEUMS AGAIN, AND WE WANT TO STOP THEM *TONIGHT!*

AND HALF AN HOUR OFF IS GOING TO *KILL* YOU?

C'MON, NIGHTINGALE -- I KNOW A NICE LITTLE *AFTER-HOURS* PLACE AROUND THE CORNER -- COULD BE YOUR *LUCKY NIGHT...*

WHAT -- QUARREL'S MAD AT YOU *AGAIN?*

AND YOU SUCH A *SENSITIVE GUY,* TOO. THE MIND POSITIVELY *BOGGLES!*

YEAH, YEAH -- SHE SAID I WAS FLIRTING WITH OTHER *WOMEN.* CAN YOU BELIEVE *IT?*

AH, LOOK AT THAT *SUNRISE!* WHAT A *GORGEOUS* SIGHT!

A FITTING FINALE TO ANOTHER *SUCCESSFUL NIGHT,* MY LAD -- AND A HARBINGER OF *MANY MORE* TO COME!

HE DEPENDS ON *LUCK,* HE IS *JEALOUS* OF OTHERS, HE DOES *SLOPPY WORK,* HE STEALS CREDIT FOR THE ACHIEVEMENTS OF *OTHERS* --

-- AND HE CALLS IT A *SUCCESSFUL NIGHT.* HE LIES EVEN TO *HIMSELF.*

HE IS NO *PARAGON.* HE IS *NOT* AN ADMIRABLE MAN.

AND YET --

AND YET --

-- WHEN OUR RACE WAS *YOUNG,* WE WERE DISMISSED AS THE *VERMIN* OF THE GALAXY, AND NOT WITHOUT *REASON.*

WE WERE *WEAK* AND *STUPID,* AND WE *LOST* EVERY WAR WE ENTERED INTO.

BUT WE NEVER *GAVE UP* -- WE NEVER STOPPED *STRIVING* --

-- AND NOW, MILLENIA LATER, WE ARE *POWERFUL* AND *RESPECTED* AND *FEARED* --

PERHAPS IT IS THAT *INDOMITABILITY* IN THESE HUMANS THAT STRIKES A CHORD WITHIN ME.

PERHAPS I SHALL REPORT THAT IT WOULD BE TOO MUCH TROUBLE TO *PACIFY* THEM -- THAT THEY WOULD RESIST BEYOND *PROFITABILITY.*

PERHAPS THIS WORLD SHALL BE *LEFT ALONE* --

-- IN THE WRECKAGE, FIREMEN DISCOVERED THE REMNANTS OF *WIGS* AND OTHER *DISGUISE MATERIALS* --

-- AND *IDENTIFICATION DOCUMENTS* IN VARIOUS NAMES.

THIS LEADS TO SPECULATION THAT *"EUGENE WALLACE"* MAY *NOT* BE THE TRUE NAME OF THE MAN BEHIND THE MASK OF --

A SURPRISING SIGN OF *RESOURCEFULNESS.* PERHAPS HE IS MORE THAN HE --

WELL, NATURALLY WE KNEW HE WAS *SOMEBODY* -- WE'VE GOT *EYES,* DON'T WE?

-- HAD MY SUSPICIONS *ALL* ALONG --

SUCH A *NICE* YOUNG MAN, TOO -- EVERYONE *LIKED* HIM --

-- BUT REALLY, THAT *WIG* --

-- NOT AS IF IT WOULD HAVE ESCAPED OUR *NOTICE* -- NOT SOMETHING THAT OUT OF THE ORDINARY --

-- NOT UNDER OUR *OWN ROOF* --

HUMANS!

SIR --

MR. BRIDWELL --

-- NOT SAFE --

HUMANS!

HUMANS!

SIGNAL IS GO. TRANSMISSION COMPLETE.

YOU ARE NOW LEAVING **ASTRO CITY** PLEASE DRIVE CAREFULLY

CHAPTER 6

THE *ZYXOMETER*, STILL WORKING IN MY OFFICE, GIVES ME THE NEWS:

THERE'S A SECURITIES HEIST IN PROGRESS AT THE *ASTRO CITY* STOCK *EXCHANGE*. A *TORNADO* THREATENING TOPEKA.

AND AN *ARMORED GIANT* WITH AN *AX* DEMANDING TRIBUTE IN CHICAGO.

BUT THE BLACK RAPIER HAS ALREADY DISABLED THE GETAWAY VEHICLES AND IS CONFRONTING THE GANG. CLEOPATRA IS DIVERTING THE TORNADO --

-- AND *REX* AND *NATALIE* OF THE *FIRST FAMILY* ARE ON THEIR WAY TO THE *WINDY CITY*.

AND *I* --

-- I HAVE NO PROBLEM WITH THE LOCK ON THE *ROOF DOOR*.

I FIND THE *APARTMENT* WITH NO DIFFICULTY.

NOK NOK

AND I WISH --

-- I WISH I WAS HEADED FOR CHICAGO *MYSELF*.

143

IT WAS A CONSPIRACY, MORE OR LESS.

NOW WE'RE NOT GOING TO TAKE NO FOR AN ANSWER, BIG GUY. YOU KEEP OVERWORKING YOURSELF LIKE THIS, YOU'RE GOING TO CRACK.

TAKE AN EVENING OFF, FOR ONCE --

-- THE REST OF US CAN KEEP THE WORLD SAFE FOR ONE NIGHT.

DID YOU TELL HIM ABOUT HIS DATE, M.P.H.?

OH, YEAH -- I ALMOST FORGOT TO MENTION...

SO WHILE M.P.H. DEALS WITH AN EASY JOB -- THE THEFT OF AN EXPERIMENTAL VEHICLE --

FASTER! FASTER! HE'S GAINING ON US!

ESTRADA PAVILION
EXOTIC AUTO SHOW TODAY

Oh, PLEASE, GUYS! THAT THING'S FAST, SURE --

-- BUT LET'S BE REALISTIC HERE -- !

-- WINGED VICTORY AND I GET AN EMPTY ROOM AND A BOUQUET OF FLOWERS...

Ah

Um

THIS IS PRICELESS, ISN'T IT? THE WORLD'S MOST PROMINENT SUPERHERO AND SUPERHEROINE, AND NEITHER OF US HAS BEEN OUT ON A DATE IN SO LONG --

-- WE'VE FORGOTTEN HOW IT WORKS.

149

SO WHILE *QUARREL*, *CRACKERJACK* AND THE *N-FORCER* HANDLE AN AVALANCHE IN MONTANA...

MY IDEA OF A *SWELL* EVENING, I'LL TELL YOU -- FREEZIN' MY *BUNS* OFF SO SOME *OTHER* GUY CAN GET *SOME!*

SHUT UP, 'JACK!

...WE END UP AT THE *BEEFY BOB'S* ON *STALLMAN STREET.*

-- NAME'S *ASA MARTIN.* I WORK AS A *FACT CHECKER* FOR *CURRENT* MAGAZINE -- THE *NEWSWEEKLY?*

REALLY? UM, NO *OFFENSE* --

IT'S *NOISY* AND *CROWDED* ENOUGH SO THAT NOBODY'S GOING TO BOTHER PAYING ATTENTION TO WHAT WE'RE *TALKING* ABOUT.

≈UF!≈

SORRY.

-- BUT IT'S NOT THE SORT OF THING I'D HAVE IMAGINED FOR YOU.

IT'S... WELL, IT'S NOT MUCH OF A *JOB*, IS IT?

I DON'T NEED THAT MUCH. THIS LETS ME TAP NEWSFEEDS WITH MY *ZYXOMETER* -- SORT OF AN ORGANIC COMPUTER --

-- AND I CAN TAKE OFF WHENEVER I *NEED* TO, AS LONG AS THE *WORK* GETS DONE...

MOO! MOO!'

WELL, YES, BUT SURELY YOU COULD GET WHATEVER CONNECTIONS YOU WANT FROM THE *GOVERNMENT* --

-- OR FROM ANY *T.V. STATION*, FOR FREE. KBAC, KACT...

I SUPPOSE I COULD, *NOW*, BUT I WOULDN'T HAVE BEEN ABLE TO WHEN I *STARTED OUT*...

...AND, WELL, I'VE BEEN KIND OF *BUSY*...

150

"...WHAT HAPPENED NEXT WAS *UNFORSEEN.*

"I DIDN'T JUST PASS *THROUGH* THE TIMESTREAM -- I WAS *SWEPT UP* IN IT -- *BUFFETED* BY IT --

"-- *SUFFUSED* WITH *EMPYREAN FIRE* -- THE PRIMAL ENERGY OF BOTH *TIME* AND *SPACE.*

"I ARRIVED IN LATE 1985 TRANSFORMED. I WAS *SEETHING* WITH ENERGY, BURSTING WITH *STRENGTH.* MY HAIR WAS A BRIGHT *BLUE*...

"...AND I WAS HOPELESSLY *OVERWHELMED.*

"THE PLAN HAD BEEN FOR ME TO CHANGE EVENTS FROM *WITHIN* -- TO INFILTRATE THE SOCIETY OF THE TIME AS AN *UNDERCOVER AGENT.*

"INSTEAD, I SPENT THE NEXT WEEKS DESPERATELY WORKING TO *CONTROL* MY NEW BODY AND ITS ABILITIES, AND HOPING I WOULDN'T RUN OUT OF *TIME.*

"I VERY NEARLY *DID.*

BIF
BIF
BIF
BIF
BIF
BIF
BIF
BIF

"ON *JANUARY 28, 1986,* THE EVENT I'D BEEN SENT TO AVERT HAPPENED: A *SEALING RING* MALFUNCTIONED DURING THE LAUNCH OF THE SPACE SHUTTLE *CHALLENGER.*

"AS A RESULT, A SOLID ROCKET BOOSTER *BROKE FREE,* CAUSING THE EXTERNAL FUEL TANK TO *EXPLODE.* THE SHIP *BROKE UP,* CRASHED INTO THE OCEAN --

"-- AND EVERYONE ABOARD WAS *KILLED.*

"OR THEY **WOULD** HAVE BEEN --"

"-- IF I HADN'T THROWN AN **EMPYREAN WEB** AROUND THE SHUTTLE AT THE LAST MOMENT --"

"-- PROTECTING THE **CREW COMPARTMENT** FROM THE BLAST, AND PREVENTING THE CRAFT FROM **BREAKING APART.**"

"IT WAS THE ONLY SOLUTION I COULD **THINK** OF, GIVEN THE **SECONDS** I HAD TO ACT --"

"-- AND THE REACTION WAS MORE THAN I WAS PREPARED FOR..."

SIR! SIR!

ARE YOU A NEW SUPERHERO? WILL YOU BE JOINING HONOR GUARD?

HOW DID YOU KNOW THERE'D BE A DISASTER? WAS IT AN **ATTACK**?

THIS WAY, SIR! WHAT'S YOUR **NAME**?!

PLEASE... I'M NOT THAT **IMPORTANT.** JUST...

...JUST CALL ME A GOOD **SAMARITAN**...

SIR! OVER HERE!

I TAPPED INTO VARIOUS COMPUTER SYSTEMS, CREATED A **DATA TRAIL** --

-- USED MY POWER TO LEACH THE **BLUE** OUT OF MY HAIR, AND GOT A JOB WHERE I COULD **INTERACT** WITH SOCIETY --

-- WHERE I COULD BUILD MYSELF A **LIFE.**

SO COME ON, DON'T STOP **THERE...**

...THEN WHAT HAPPENED?

Oh, I'M *SORRY*... YOUR *FAMILY*... YOUR WHOLE WORLD...

IT'S OKAY. WE KNEW GOING INTO IT THAT THIS WOULD PROBABLY HAPPEN IF I WAS *SUCCESSFUL*, AND WE ALL AGREED THAT --

'SCUSE.

DON'T THINK TWICE ABOUT IT, I'M SURE.

AND IN *SAN FRANCISCO* --

WRAK

YES! SHE GOT HIM!

YOU MEAN *BEAUTIE* AND *GOLDENBOY*, RIGHT?

HOW DID YOU -- ?

ZYXOMETER TERMINAL IMPLANTED IN MY *EARLOBE*. THERE'S A COP CALLING THE NEWS IN FROM HIS *SQUAD CAR*, AND IT'S BEING ROUTED TO ME.

WITH ME, IT'S MY *MEDALLION*, I DON'T ALWAYS GET HARD FACTS, BUT I PICK UP *IMAGES*...

WE'RE A COUPLE OF *WORKAHOLICS,* IT SEEMS -- ADDICTED TO OUR *BEEPERS.*

HEY, I'LL TURN MINE OFF IF YOU TURN *YOURS* OFF.

POINT TAKEN.

STILL, I WISH I'D BEEN ABLE TO GET GOLDENBOY *MYSELF.* THE WAY HE USES HIS ENHANCED CHARISMA TO *ENSNARE* WOMEN...

...I'D LIKE TO HAVE MADE HIM *EAT* THAT SMIRK OF HIS...

IT'S *FUNNY* -- BUT, WELL, *I'VE* FOUGHT GOLDENBOY TOO, AND JUST NOW I WAS THINKING OF HIM AS "*YOUR*" VILLAIN.

THE SAME WITH *FEVER* AND A *FEW* OTHERS. WHY *IS* THAT -- SHOULDN'T IT BE JUST THE LUCK OF THE DRAW?

NO, IT'S *DELIBERATE CHOICE,* AT LEAST ON MY PART. I CONCENTRATE ON PROTECTING *WOMEN* -- -- OR ON DEMONSTRATING THAT WOMEN DON'T AUTOMATICALLY NEED MEN TO *SHIELD* THEM.

SO I *TARGET* JERKS LIKE GOLDEN-BOY.

WAIT A MINUTE. SAY YOU'VE GOT A MAN FALLING TO HIS DEATH *HERE,* AND A WOMAN DROWNING *THERE.*

YOU'D *IGNORE* THE MAN TO SAVE THE WOMAN? *CONSCIOUSLY?*

ALL OTHER THINGS BEING EQUAL... *YES.*

BUT... *WHY?*

159

BUT *EVERYBODY* NEEDS TO STEP BACK, TO GET SOME *PERSPECTIVE,* EVEN IF IT'S JUST IN YOUR --

BUT YOU WOULDN'T NEED THAT.

ACTUALLY, I DON'T CHANGE BACK TO MY NORMAL FORM THAT *OFTEN.* I LIVE AT ONE OF THE *SCHOOLS* --

-- THE APARTMENT I MET YOU AT BELONGS TO ONE OF OUR *ACCOUNTANTS.*

-- GEEZ, IT'S COMING UP ON *TWO* YEARS NOW...

YOU MUST HAVE *FAMILY,* FRIENDS TO TURN TO -- FROM *BEFORE?*

I DON'T THINK I'VE BEEN BACK TO MY *HOMETOWN,* OR SEEN MY *MOM,* IN --

REALLY?

WOW -- YOU'RE ALMOST AS CUT OFF AS I AM -- !

POUR IT ON! *POUR IT ON!*

AN' DON'T HOLD BACK ON *MY* ACCOUNT! I CAN KEEP THIS *COCKAMAMIE THING* TOGETHER TILL *GUS* AND *MR. SWORDO* HIT THE RIGHT *WAVELENGTH!*

ASTRA! YOU *READY,* HONEY?

KRIK

AND
THEN --

-- AND THEN A *SILENT ALARM* GOES OFF AT A TOP-SECURITY LAB IN *PALO ALTO* --

LOOK, I'VE GOT TO --

YEAH, I SHOULD DEAL WITH THIS -- THIS *THING* HAPPENING NEAR SEKOWSKY STREET --

AND JUST BEFORE I'M OUT OF RANGE, I HEAR HER LAUGH QUIETLY TO HERSELF, AND WHISPER, *"THERE'S ALWAYS HOPE."*

"THERE'S *ALWAYS* HOPE."

WELL, THERE *IS.*

YOU ARE NOW LEAVING **ASTRO CITY** PLEASE DRIVE CAREFULLY

INFRASTRUCTURE

City Planning

Creating an entire city from the ground up, one with over 75 years of superhero history, isn't the easiest of challenges. When you've got one writer and two artists (three, if you count Art Nichols's lettercolumn cityscape), you can't just make things up as you go along. Everything's got to be worked out in advance — and while at times, I feel like Alex, Brent and I are burying each other under continual round-robin faxes, with revisions of this and designs for that, it's been a major thrill to see this world come to life, neighborhood by neighborhood and sketch by sketch.

— Kurt Busiek

Below ▼ Brent's notes on how to draw the "rocket" beacon atop the AstroBank tower — based on a two-dimensional design by Alex, which was in turn inspired by faxes I sent him of the old, discontinued library-system genre-sticker for "science fiction."

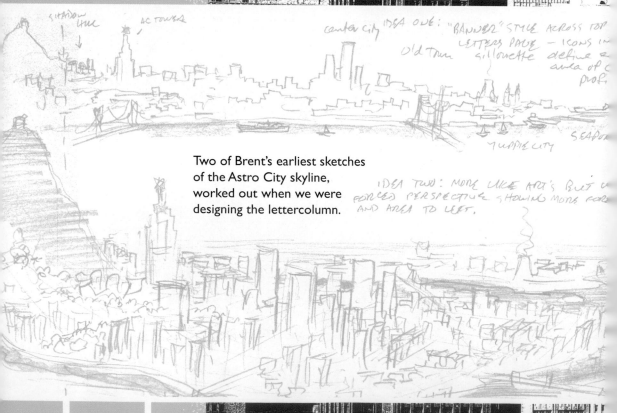

"ELECTRON" PATHS MEET AT TWO POINTS 90° TO THE ROCKET & AT 45° TO THE UPRIGHT

ROCKET LENGTH FROM NOSE TO FIN TIPS PRECISELY FITS INTO SPHERE OF "ELECTRON" ORBITS (IT'S IN PERSPECTIVE ON THIS SHOT SO LOOKS A LITTLE SHORT)

ROCKET ANGLED UPWARD @ 45° TO THE UPRIGHT, AND 45° TO ORIENTATION OF BUILDING.

UP

FIN ARRANGEMENT

ROCKET IS ORIENTED AT 45° TO THE BUILDING.

BUILDING IS SAME DESIGN FRONT TO BACK AND SIDE TO SIDE.

SHADOW HILL
AC TOWERS

Center City IDEA ONE: "BANNER" STYLE ACROSS TOP
Old Town LETTERS PAGE — ICONS IN
silhouette define &
area of c
profi

SEAPOR

YUPPIE CITY

Two of Brent's earliest sketches of the Astro City skyline, worked out when we were designing the lettercolumn.

IDEA TWO: MORE LIKE ART'S BUT W
FORCED PERSPECTIVE SHOWING MORE FOR
AND AREA TO LEFT.

City Planning

In the inset is my very first rough map (and rough it is indeed!) of Astro City and its environs, and below, Brent's reworking of it into something that looks more like an actual city. This is very early — we hadn't named the rivers or most of the neighborhoods yet, the prison island got a new name by the time #1 got lettered, and we added some stuff here and there — but it's got all the basics.

Samaritan

Some of Alex's dozens (hundreds?) of sketches working out a design for Samaritan, showing the development of his chest-symbol and some attempts to figure out a distinctive cape. The cape design we finally went with is an extreme stylization of a Greek toga.

THIN GOLD TRIM ON CAPE?

Samaritan

Facial studies of Samaritan. Even if Alex was painting him on the cover to #1 with his face obscured, Brent had to draw him all through the issue, so Alex worked out his face from many angles to make sure he and Brent would be drawing exactly the same man.

COLORATION

HAS CAPE

FIND OUT WHAT HER PERSONAL SYMBOL IS

CLOTH GORE GLOVES

UPSIDE DOWN SHIELD SHAPE

DRAW CHAIN MAIL THIS WAY →

CHAIN MAIL IS BLUE-GRAY

CLOTH LEGS AND BOOTS

LEGS BARE NO CHAIN MAIL

CHAIN MAIL GOES UNDER HELMET AND COVERS ARMS AND BECOMES TRUNKS

Upper right ◀
Three designs for Cleopatra. The one furthest left is striking and memorable, but it didn't quite say "hero" to me. The two others became the modern Cleopatra and the 1959 Cleopatra respectively.

Above, ▲ and lower right ▶
Early sketches for the Silver Agent, including variant helmet and chest-shield ideas

Handwritten annotations (left sketch):

HELMET & CHEST-PIECE → METAL

BRENT: THIS IS THE BASIC N-FORCE IDEA, BUT DON'T [...] THESE DETAILS [...]

SOME SORT OF DEFINED SHOULDER

← FACE IS ENER[...]

ARMS A[...] E[...] ENE[...]

GLOVES METAL →

PELVIS & BOOTS METAL

MIDRIFF: ENERGY OR METAL?

ALEX SUGGESTS WORKING OUT 1964 VERSION (CLUNKY, CRUDE) AND 1995 VERSION (SLEEK, HI-TECH) SIMULTANEOUSLY FOR THEMATIC COHERENCE.

[THIS VERSION: BAD 1974 VERSION?]

THIS KIND OF STYLE WOULD NEED TO BE TOUCHED UP SO AS NOT TO APPEAR TOO SIMILAR TO X-O MANOWAR

MAYBE WITHOUT NOSE COVER

STILL VERY "IRON-MANNISH"

SHOW MORE OF FACE THOUGH

-KUR

ANGLED EYES?

SPIDEY EYES

WIDER EYE OPENINGS?

CHIN GUARD?

R.W. 3-13-95 3-29-95

LEGS [...] ARMS UNDER[...]

Honor Guard

We spent so much time on the N-Forcer — a character who has yet to be much more than a walk-on — that we could have filled this entire section with nothing but rejected sketches of him. Here are a few of them, including **Left ◄** my hideous concept sketch **Below ▼** the sketch by Alex that got us on the right track, and **Below Left ▼** a variant design of Brent's.

Many of the different N-Forcer designs below will turn up as incarnations of his armor over the decades. Don't worry — we didn't do this much work to leave him in the background forever...

Honor Guard

More Honor Guard designs: *To the right* ▶ Brent's original sketch of Quarrel, and a suggestion for revised leggings from Alex. *Below, counterclockwise from bottom left* ▼ My original sketch for Starwoman (you can see now why I work with professionals…), Brent's design sketches for Beautie, with Alex's mask suggestions, . *Opposite page, top* Brent's initial sketch for M.P.H. and the final design.

I CAME FROM PLANET CLAIRE!

174

For MPH's suit
Imagine a
cross between
a 1960's style
Le Mans racing
car and a
dolphin - shiney,
sleek, smooth.
(Has the feel of
a car racer's
fire suit)

cuff to body suit

← Racing gloves

His boots are
reminiscent of
Red Ball Jets high-
top sneakers.

Jack-in-the-Box

Jack-in-the-Box didn't quite gel visually until Alex and I were sitting in a little Italian restaurant in New York after a convention, sketching on napkins and arguing, to the amusement of Ray Lago, Jordan Raskin and the other diners. The concept clicked when we hit on the stylized clown eyes and giving him "Bozo hair" as a collar that would frame his head without touching it. From there, Alex went to town on the guy, producing one of the most striking designs of the whole series.

JACK-IN-THE-BOX

RED LIPS

RED HAIR

GREEN & RED DIAMOND PATTERN

GREEN & RED "SPRING SURPRISE" PUNCHING ARM

YELLOW MISTER MIRACLE-STYLE KIRBY DISCS

GREEN BAG

RED PANTS

GREEN & RED

E ven "cannon fodder"
has to be designed —
this is Brent's design drawing of one of Shirak's
"devourers," drawn to help Alex paint the cover to #2.

BROAD
MUSCULAR
BACKS

— SHARK
HEAD THRUSTS
FROM SHOULDER
GIRDLE

5 GILL SLITS UNDER
EACH ARM

SHARP
"THUMBS" THAT
DON'T FLEX

TWO
FINGERS
SHARP INDEX

SQUARED OFF
2nd FINGER

FAIRLY THICK
WAIST

SCALEY
TOUGH-LOOKING
HIDE w/PADDED
SCALE PATTERN
ON KNEES AND
ELBOWS

SHARK MEN
ASTRO CITY #2
5 3-95

NARROW ANKLES

4 TOED
FEET

SQUARED OFF

WRINKLES
AROUND
MOUTH

POINTY

YOU
CAN USE
WIDE LATITUDE
IN UNIQUE PRO-
PORTIONS OF
INDIVIDUAL
SHARK MEN

PECTORALS AND
ABDOMINUS ERECTUS FORM
A SERIES OF PLATE-LIKE
OVERLAPPING FORMS

First Family

Across the top ◄ Initial design ideas for the First Family's uniforms, starting with something too "Star Trek: The Next Generation" and getting closer to what we finally used.

A GRIFFIN

REX!

OSCAR!

REX!

All we knew about Rex of the First Family, when we started out, was that he'd be married to Dr. Furst's adoptive daughter Natalie, he'd be a monster, and he'd be the son of one of the team's arch-enemies. We tried lots of different concepts, from a lion-man to a gryphon to a rock-creature, but nothing clicked ...

...until we realized that the name "Rex," originally invented during the "lion man" stage, could apply as easily to a tyrannosaur. After that, it was easy.

All sketches on this page are by Alex.

177

Ordinary People

Some of the "little people," sketched by Alex to co-ordinate his cover paintings with what Brent drew in the interior art, plus reference photos shot by Alex for the covers.

WIRE RIM GLASSES

30'S GRAYISH

MY SUGGESTION FOR SAMARITAN'S HAIR IS CURLY INSTEAD OF STRAIGHT BRINGS. THIS GIVES A MORE JEWISH FEEL AND DEFINITELY CLASHES WITH HIS SUPERHERO HAIR. THIS WAY WHEN HE PUTS HIS FINGERS THROUGH HIS HAIR HE IS STRAIGHTENING IT AND SLICKING IT BACK AS IT CHANGES COLOR.

MEDIUM SIZE NOSE PERKED UP A LITTLE →

LIGHT THIN EYEBROWS

UNDRAMATIC EYES

5'8"

LIT CIG. OFTEN

RECESSIVE CHIN

THIN BUT STRONG NECK

SOFT 50'S HAIRCUT BLACK

WIRE FRAMES

WIDE SPACE BETWEEN NOSE AND MOUTH

THIS IS PRETTY MUCH WHAT MARTA LOOKS LIKE ON THE COVER OF #4 SHE IS WEARING A NAVY BLUE BUSINESS COAT WHICH IS FOLDED AT THE CUFF AROUND MID-FOREARM

YOU SHOULD DEFINITELY SEE THAT COVER BEFORE YOU GO ANY FARTHER.

EYEBROWS ARE A LITTLE BUSHY BUT NOT OVERLY SO.

EYES ARE SOMEWHAT CLOSE-SET.

From the top down ▲ Asa "Samaritan" Martin from #1 and #6 (we changed his hair, but kept the face the same), Eliot Mills from #2, and Marta from #4.

YOU NEEDN'T GO WITH THIS EXACTLY IF WHAT YOU DO ROUGHLY PASSES FOR THE COVER FACE. I WAS THINKING OF KIND OF A NATASHA KINSKI LOOK FOR ETHNICITY AND I DIDN'T WIND UP GETTING THAT BUT ONCE YOU SEE THE COVER I'M SURE YOU'LL HAVE OTHER IDEAS.

WHITE SHIRT

NAVY BLUE SPORTCOAT

COVER GALLERY

DON'T MISS THE REST OF THE ASTRO CITY SERIES:

ABOUT THE CREATORS

KURT BUSIEK broke into comics in 1982, selling stories to both DC and Marvel within weeks of finishing college. Since then, he's been an editor, a literary agent, a sales manager and more, but is best known as the multiple-award-winning writer of ASTRO CITY, MARVELS, SUPERMAN, CONAN, ARROWSMITH, SUPERSTAR, SHOCKROCKETS and many others. He lives in the Pacific Northwest with his family.

STEVE BUCCELLATO fancies himself a master of visual communication! Whatever that means. As a writer & artist, editor and occasional self-publisher, Steve likes to mix things up. However, he's still probably best known for his award-winning comic book coloring, which you may appreciate in this lovely book, which remains one of his favorites.

BRENT ANDERSON began writing and drawing his own comics in junior high school, and graduated to professional work less than a decade later. He's drawn such projects as KA-ZAR THE SAVAGE, X-MEN: GOD LOVES MAN KILLS, STRIKEFORCE: MORITURI, SOMERSET HOLMES, RISING STARS and, of course, ASTRO CITY, for which he's won multiple Eisner and Harvey Awards. He makes his home in Northern California.

JOHN G. ROSHELL joined Comicraft in 1992, helping propel the lettering/design studio to its dominant position in the industry. As Senior Design Wizard, he's lettered thousands of comics pages, along with creating logos and fonts, designing book editions and more. He also writes the series CHARLEY LOVES ROBOTS, which appears in ELEPHANTMEN.

ALEX ROSS worked on TERMINATOR: THE BURNING EARTH and Clive Barker's HELLRAISER before his breakout series, MARVELS, made him an overnight superstar. Since then, he's painted, plotted and/or written such series as KINGDOM COME, SUPERMAN: PEACE ON EARTH, JUSTICE, EARTH X, AVENGERS/INVADERS and PROJECT SUPERPOWERS, and won over two dozen industry awards.

RICHARD STARKINGS dimly remembers working on some BATMAN project... THE KILLING JOKE? People insist that he did letter it with a tool not unlike a computer... but too many lattes and British chocolate has wiped his recollections of anything prior to Illustrator 5. He currently writes ELEPHANTMEN.